M000003397

John-Paul Flintoff is a feature writer for Britain's best-selling upmarket newspaper, *The Sunday Times*. He has also written for the *Financial Times*, *The Guardian*, *The New Statesman*, *Esquire*, *Harpers Bazaar* and – well, lots of other publications.

As well as writing, he has worked as bin man, executive PA, scuba diver, poet, taxi driver, tailor, gardener, ice-cream salesman, film-maker, assistant undertaker, bit-part player in pantomime, waiter, illustrator, high-wire window cleaner, photographer, very amateur boxer, karaoke singer and rat catcher.

His writing has attracted compliments from the documentary maker Michael Moore, the stage and film director Richard Eyre, and the late Nobel-winner Harold Pinter ("Very good. Very funny ... In fact, it made me laugh").

Flintoff's memoir, *Comp: A Survivor's Tale*, attracted huge media attention on its publication, and praise from an assortment of admirable and intelligent people, including Francis Wheen, Cristina Odone and Vanessa Feltz.

PRAISE FOR

Comp: A Survivor's Tale

"Makes *The Lord of The Flies* look like a soft-soap cover-up." - *The Guardian*

"A light-footed comic autobiography." - *The Big Issue*

"Flintoff has not written a history of Holland Park Comprehensive, though he has woven the essential historical facts into his narrative. He has done something far more rewarding and entertaining, turning his rite de passage, from cocky middle-class product of the polite Fox Junior School to case-hardened young offender, into a very funny memoir... Comp is a marvellous account of growing up rough in West London." - *Times Literary Supplement*

"Often hilarious... the timing of a natural." - *The Sunday Times*

"An entertaining and thoughtful memoir... manages to be funny while making a serious point... [Flintoff] conveys the blatant hostility of the less privileged, the chaos of adolescent lust, and the comedy of classroom anarchy, while acknowledging the treacherous cruelty of which teenagers are capable. There may be a lesson here, but Flintoff is the gentlest of moralists." - *Financial Times*

"I hope John-Paul Flintoff is a fast runner. He'll need to be if his old classmates at Holland Park Comprehensive ever find him. Flintoff has written an hilariously merciless memoir." - *Metro*

"Very readable, in an Adrian Mole-possessed-by-Satan kind of way." - *The Spectator*

"The first time the lid has been lifted on the school once dubbed the 'Eton of comprehensives'." - *The Evening Standard*

"Unmissable." - *Catholic Herald*

"It has faint echoes of the tender bravado of Salinger's Catcher in the Rye and gives a nod to the wicked young Amis of The Rachel Papers. But mostly Flintoff writes as his own likeable, transparent self." - *New Statesman*

"It all rings too horribly, comically true." - *Glasgow Herald*

"Comp is a compendium of teenage delinquency... the great strength of the book – which is often funny in the blackest way imaginable – is its non-judgmental frankness." - *Times Educational Supplement*

"A fun and honest book." - *Literary Review*

"Hilarious, hair-raising narrative... manages to be both supremely entertaining and an invaluable social document. The closing "register" of what happened to Flintoff's old school friends is priceless." - *Daily Telegraph*

"I thought that at worst this book would give the reader a rough idea of what the British education system was about. That was what it gave me.. and then some more. I haven't laughed out loud reading a book in a while." - *Amazon Reader Review*

Through the eye of a needle

John-Paul Flintoff

Permanent Publications

www.permaculture.co.uk

Published by

THE QUEEN'S AWARDS
FOR ENTERPRISE:
SUSTAINABLE DEVELOPMENT
2008

Permanent Publications
Hyden House Ltd
The Sustainability Centre
East Meon
Hampshire GU32 1HR
United Kingdom
Tel: 01730 823 311
Fax: 01730 823 322
Overseas: (international code +44 - 1730)
Email: enquiries@permaculture.co.uk
Web: www.permaculture.co.uk

Published in association with

Permaculture Association (Britain)
Tel: 0845 458 1805 Email: office@permaculture.org.uk Web: www.permaculture.org.uk

© 2009 John-Paul Flintoff

The right of John-Paul Flintoff to be identified as the author of this work has been
asserted by him in accordance with the Copyrights, Designs and Patents Act 1998

Illustrations and photographs by John-Paul Flintoff unless otherwise indicated.
Cover design by Joe McAllister.

Designed by Two Plus George Limited, www.TwoPlusGeorge.co.uk

FSC
Mixed Sources
Product group from well-managed
forests and other controlled sources
Cert no. SGS-COC-2953
www.fsc.org
© 1996 Forest Stewardship Council

Printed in the UK by CPI Antony Rowe,
Chippenham, Wiltshire

All paper from FSC certified mixed sources

The Forest Stewardship Council (FSC) is a non-profit
international organisation established to promote the responsible
management of the world's forests. Products carrying the FSC
label are independently certified to assure consumers that they
come from forests that are managed to meet the social, economic
and ecological needs of present and future generations.

British Library Cataloguing-in-Publication Data
A catalogue record for this book is available from the British Library

ISBN 978 1 85623 045 2

All rights reserved. No part of this publication may be reproduced, stored in a
retrieval system, rebound or transmitted in any form or by any means, electronic,
mechanical, photocopying, recording or otherwise, without the prior permission
of Hyden House Limited.

Through the Eye of a Needle

One man's attempt to survive economic meltdown, tackle climate change, and enter the kingdom of heaven — by making his own clothes

By John-Paul Flintoff

INCLUDING: why his *wife* won't always allow him to <u>wear</u> his home-made clothes in **public**

AND: his journey, as a lifelong unbeliever, through various <u>Christian</u> churches, in a search for the right fit for his soul, and encounters with *Buddhists*

++++++++++++++++++++++++++++++++++

PLUS: a similar journey across the political spectrum, leading him to disillusionment, *and finally to a determination to do whatever needs doing himself, of which* **clothes-making** *is only one example, the others including tackling terrorism,* <u>economic revival</u> *through barter, and managing pest control*

FEATURING: film stars **Richard Gere** and *Daryl Hannah*, politicians and campaigners, criminals and priests, the Victorian essayist <u>John Ruskin</u>, injured New York-based sweatshop operatives, British TV's celebrated petrol-head **Jeremy Clarkson** and the anti-road protestor who stuck a pie in his face, members of the ancient guild of spinners, dyers and weavers, the Quaker philanthropist *Elizabeth Fry*, call-centre workers in Bangalore, the author's wife's 98-year-old great aunt *Peggy Parker*, a "naked yoga" teacher, Prince Charles's own Savile Row tailor, a "personal shopper", the German army of the First World War, **Mahatma Gandhi**, the *Buddha*, <u>Jesus Christ</u> and Vivienne Westwood.

CONTENTS

PART TWO

How many angels
Admiring my handiwork
Dance on this pin's end!

PROLOGUE

I'm sitting on the Northern Line, on the City branch, in the middle of rush hour, on a carriage crowded with people dressed in smart clothes, with expensive accessories.

I used to be just like these people, and wore the same kind of clothes.

Not any more.

These days I tend to wear home-made. Today, every item of clothing on me has either been made from scratch, or significantly modified or repaired.

Not that I would expect you to notice: indeed, I try to make the clothes look just as good as the ones I used to buy. If I didn't, my wife might not let me out of the house in them.

But there's no point making clothes yourself and keeping it secret. Not if you want the whole world to start doing the same. Not if you believe, as I do, that home-made, locally sourced clothes are as important to the survival of our species as home-grown, locally sourced food; and similarly good for your wallet at a time when the economy is in collapse. Not if you believe that the act of making clothes is its own reward – an outlet for creativity and empowerment that used to be enjoyed by every person on the planet.

I didn't come to these conclusions overnight, or by myself. I can't even begin to count the number of people who influenced me, including some you would hardly believe, such as Jeremy Clarkson. But the one who's at the forefront of my mind as I sit on this train is Gandhi. He predicted that if Indians learned to grow their own plants and spun and wove the fibres into cloth themselves, and used that to make their own clothes, they would destroy the British cotton industry and ultimately overthrow the British Empire. And he was right.

"Be the change you want to see in the world," Gandhi said. And he did it too: not only wearing homespun clothes but actually taking his spinning wheel to political meetings.

Me, I don't have a spinning wheel – yet.

But I do have a crochet hook. It's hidden in the pocket of my jacket. In the other pocket, I've got some yarn.

I look around me casually at the passengers who pretend, as ever, not to be looking at each other. I know that they are looking really, surreptitiously glancing at anything out of the ordinary. Do I dare to take out the hook, and the yarn, and Be the Change…?

PART
ONE

chapter 1

*In which the author jets across the Atlantic
to be fitted for a suit by a robot, and road-
tests an off-the-peg "washable suit"*

Where does a revolution begin? The French revolution didn't
begin at the guillotine: that was more like the end. The Russian
revolution, similarly, started long before Lenin returned home
from exile. And the local, home-made clothing revolution?

My own part in it began several years ago, quite improbably,
with a flight across the Atlantic.

Like many other people at the time – the turn of the millennium,
amid a dotcom bubble that was yet to burst – I was dazzled by
high-tech. For this reason, when I flew to New York for work I
took myself to an upmarket clothing store to be measured for a
suit by lasers.

It's fair to say that what I learned on the day had little global
significance. For instance, I discovered that, besides having defects
that were immediately apparent, my body was imperfect in ways I
could hardly have guessed at.

The lights cast by the digital scanner captured approximately
200,000 body measurements in less than five seconds. This revealed that my right shoulder is more than half an inch lower than
my left. My neck is too thick – and shoulders too broad – for my
narrow frame. I had a vague notion of this beforehand because
off-the-peg outfits, if they fitted at the neck and shoulders, tended
to be baggy. Now I knew for sure.

During the scan, which took place in the privacy of a felt-lined
chamber, the customer is encouraged by a pre-recorded female
voice and further assisted, from outside, by a human assistant
communicating by headset. As the measurements came through,
they were converted by computer into a virtual mannequin. And

when the scan had finished, the customer stepped outside and started putting together a custom-made suit fitted exactly to his quirky body shape.

Naturally, there are issues to resolve before buying a suit, which in the "digital tailoring" department at Brooks Brothers cost between $700 and $1,300. Side vents? Belt loops? Back pockets? Plain cloth or check? The assistants know better than most customers – better than me, anyway – which shapes and fabrics suit any given body shape.

The finished outfit, I was promised, would be ready in a fortnight. Additional orders could be placed by phone or email. The virtual mannequin would remain on the store's computer forever – or until the customer, gaining or losing sensational quantities of weight, needed scanning anew.

I liked the system so much I ordered two suits. Additionally, the human assistant with the headset very kindly threw in a free shirt – only, he regretted that this would be available only in one of two fabrics left over in surplus. Neither colour particularly appealed to me, but the shirt was free and I opted for the least bad, a slatey blue that I suspected might give me a rather sickly pallor.

Some weeks later, the shirt and the suits arrived in London in big parcels, on which I had incidentally to pay a substantial amount in tax.

I tried them on. The coats on the suits seemed extraordinarily long and boxy, but in other respects the fit was excellent. As for the shirt – well, if you haven't worn a fitted shirt you just don't know what you're missing. It feels fantastic, extraordinarily comfortable, rather like a second skin. Certainly an awful lot better than the hot air-balloons I'd been buying at Thomas Pink, each one costing a small fortune.

But as I had guessed, the colour of the Brooks Brothers shirt didn't suit me. My wife disliked it, and she absolutely hated the suits. The long coats, Harriet announced, looked very odd indeed.

I find it hard to wear something after Harriet has told me she dislikes it. There's an uncomfortable feeling, similar to carrying on watching comedy on TV after she has asked, "Do you really think this is funny?" Her dim view of my new clothes was extremely demoralising, not least because altogether I had spent several hundred pounds.

For what it's worth, I know that Harriet has my interests at heart. OK, she has her own interests at heart, because she doesn't relish being seen with somebody dressed peculiarly, or badly, but she does also sincerely not want me to look bad even when she's not there.

This explains why, after several years, I have worn the fitted shirt fewer than five times, and never worn either of my Brooks Brothers suits – not once. Well, not for more than five minutes every couple of years, when I try them on to see whether they are really as bad as we thought – and they still are.

What I tend to wear instead, if I wear a suit at all – which is extremely rare now that I no longer work in an office – is a cheap off-the-peg suit I bought at Marks & Spencer three years later because it was sold as machine-washable.

If suits were easy to clean, I thought at the time, perhaps I would wear them all the time – transforming my image from scruffy heap to suave James Bond type?

I was aware that men who have young children get their suits dirty all the time, because babies chuck up on them, and because I was about to become a father I was trying to make space in my budget for a dramatically larger dry-cleaning bill.

A washable suit, it seemed obvious, would reduce that expense.

So I ordered one in navy blue with narrow white pinstripes. (It cost £125; and was also available in black, with a dinner suit for slightly more money.) When it arrived I was impressed. Of course, it didn't fit as well as the bespoke ones – the jacket was slightly loose around the back – but that seemed an acceptable trade-off.

To test the suit properly, I wore it for a few days to the office of the newspaper where I then worked, to unrestrained expressions of surprise from colleagues more used to seeing me in jeans. I wore it on trains, aeroplanes and taxis as I travelled to interview, among others, a de facto head of state and a representative of Russia's imperial family in exile.

Neither of those eminent figures looked askance at the suit, perhaps because they were unable to detect by eye alone the considerable proportion of artificial fibres in the wool blend. (But then, one of these men wore jeans and the other told me M&S was his favourite tailor, so they could hardly sniff.)

The only person who found it hard to conceal his disapproval for the suit was my wife's brother; but Daniel has, in this respect, exquisite tastes. To him, M&S's professed commitment to "making aspirational quality available to everyone" could in itself be considered a bad thing. Certainly the low price would be regarded as an embarrassment among the surveyors, bankers and ad execs with whom Daniel transacts his working life.

Still, after several days, the suit still wasn't dirty enough. I made a few calls. My nephew, one-year-old Zachary Brown, gave me to understand that he was happy to help out: we could muck about in the garden, perhaps eat ice cream together. He hinted that if I came round after four, when his older brothers Joseph and Reuben got back from swimming, they might be willing to help too.

I turned up as agreed, accompanied by the *Financial Times* photographer Charlie Bibby (my washable suit had made such an impression, I'd been asked to write about it). The children dutifully jumped on me, at Charlie's request, and Zac tirelessly dabbled his finger in ice cream to smear it on my lapels.

So far as it went, this seemed satisfactory. But Charlie felt that the suit still didn't look particularly dirty. With a glint in his eye he said it might help if I checked the oil in his car and gave it a quick wash. I knew what he was up to – getting a free carwash – but did as he requested, even allowing the front of the jacket to sweep through the soapy lather on the bonnet.

On the faces of passers-by, I could read the following question: "Why is that man cleaning his car in his suit?" The answer – "because I can" – would seem to confirm that M&S has created a sartorial item of real value, if possibly a little niche. Certainly, this alone couldn't account for the company's boast that washable suits had become bestsellers.

I took the suit home, stuffed it inside the conveniently supplied washing net, and shoved the whole lot in the machine at 40 degrees. Afterwards, I shook it vigorously and hung it up to dry. By the next morning the suit was dry and largely – though not entirely – free of creases. (The ones down the front of the trousers, which are supposed to be there, still were.)

chapter 2

*Meeting sweat-shop workers in New York,
the author fails even for a second to consider
that his own clothes might be made by people
in similar conditions*

Five years later, the washable suit is still in good nick. But I don't
like it any more than the ones from Brooks Brothers. This may
sound odd, if you've not yet experienced what I've experienced, but
I don't like any of those suits because I don't know who made them,
and I don't believe that love went into the making of them – at
£125, how could it?

How was this not apparent to me before? Why did it not bother
me then? I don't know, but for reasons that I hope will gradually
become clear, I have no more interest in sneering at my younger
self, or finding fault with him, than I have in sneering at you, or
anybody else.

And here I'm going to offer a rather bold analogy: did Paul,
moving on from the Road to Damascus, waste time sneering at
people from whose eyes the scales had yet to fall? Did the Buddha,
sitting under the Bodhi tree, find fault with others who had yet to
become enlightened? I think you will find they didn't.

But it *is* rather astonishing how blinkered I was – because
while in New York to be measured up by lasers I was researching a
magazine story about people making clothes in sweat shops right
there in Manhattan.

I met several of the people involved. People like Lilia Luna,
who had arrived in New York 12 years earlier, from Mexico, and
immediately found work in a garment factory. That lasted a year,
until she became pregnant. Then she got a job at a building on

West 38th Street, on the sixth floor, making clothes for Donna Karan.

Sixty women worked there, making evening gowns, jackets and coats. The loos were padlocked: workers could use them only after finishing their quota of work. Phones were not allowed. Surveillance cameras monitored the workers' movements. Paid holidays and maternity leave did not exist. Even when workers requested unpaid time off it was commonly refused. Long hours at work – often 11 hours a day, six days a week – affected the women's health. Most suffered neck, back, shoulder and leg pains. Meanwhile, their families suffered. One woman discovered that her son had been skipping school – but by the time she found out, he'd been doing it for a year.

Additionally, there was discrimination. Chinese Americans used sewing machines, Latin Americans stitched by hand. "The boss would say Latinas were not good with machines," Luna said. "She said we would break them."

Having always worked alongside Spanish speakers, she learned little English. When I met her at her apartment in Harlem – amid gaudy images of the Virgin and frequent interventions from her youngest daughter – she spoke through an interpreter. Her manner was modest, she spoke quietly: it took time to get out of her how dreadful the job was.

Earnings were calculated on a piece rate, depriving workers of payments such as time-and-a-half for working more than 40 hours a week. And with complex, time-consuming garments, piece rate amounted to less than the minimum wage. "I was surprised to see how expensive the clothes were," Luna told me. "Sometimes we would talk to each other and say, 'How come these jackets are so expensive but we get paid so little?'"

Luna was one of several workers suing Donna Karan over conditions in the factory. Like the others, she would never be able to launch such a case alone. Adam Klein, the lawyer representing them, explained that his firm, Outten & Golden, was taking a risk and would only be paid if the case succeeded. "Individual workers can't pay for this. And we can't take on a case like this unless it's a class action. You have to be doing it for all the workers together.

"There is a lot at stake for these folks, personally," he said. "They are concerned about retaliation. Many don't speak English and a lot are undocumented" – not entitled to live and work in the US. "This is another reason they're easy to exploit."

Donna Karan's initial response to the lawsuit was a short statement asserting the company's concern, and revealing a "factory compliance program" to promote improved working conditions. Subsequently, Donna Karan brought a motion to dismiss the case, arguing it was not directly responsible because the factory was run by a contractor, Chung Suk Choe. But that motion was itself dismissed. "The work was extensively for DKNY," Klein explained. And Karan's reps were fully aware of conditions in the factory. "We saw the reps every day," said Luna. "They would check the clothing that was finished and maybe look at how we were working. Then they would talk to the manager." And the manager would pass on their demands to workers. "Their comments were very detailed."

Altogether, some 93,000 people worked in clothes manufacturing in New York when I was there to research that story, and the Department of Labour estimated that more than half the 7,500 garment factories should be classed as sweatshops. "Most sweatshop activism in this country is about factories overseas. But people walk by New York's sweatshops every day," said Karah Newton, of the Brooklyn-based National Mobilisation Against Sweat Shops. "The US model is one of the most brutal systems for keeping people working," she adds. Another activist, Betty Yu, said: "In other countries people are shot. Well, they don't shoot people here because they want to keep you working."

Newton and Yu introduced me to many other aggrieved and injured workers, including You Di Liao, a former rice farmer from China, who collapsed at another garment factory after working too many 16-hour days on her feet.

I was fascinated to learn that there were sweatshops in New York. I thought they only existed in poor countries. And I wasn't the only one.

Five women, including Liao, flew to Mexico City to file a claim on behalf of 13 New York-based immigrants, accusing the Workers Compensation Board of routinely stalling on workers' claims – in contravention of the North American Free Trade Agreement between Canada, the US and Mexico. They could have posted it, but going to Mexico was more likely to win them publicity – a crucial part of their strategy.

"We arrived on Tuesday night and went straight to a hotel," recalls Ranjana Natarajan, a clinical fellow at NYU who accompanied them. To keep costs to a minimum, the five shared two rooms. On Wednesday, they took a taxi to file the petition at the National Administrative Office. Afterwards, on the pavement, they held a press conference. There were reporters from *The New York Times*, TV and Mexican newspapers. Also present were workers camped out in tents, who had been laid off by a Mexican company. "It was startling to them to hear about our problems in the US. They said, 'We didn't know…' The impression was that in the US, because it's such a rich country, there would be no problems like this and the law would be better enforced."

Looking back, I find it astonishing that it didn't even occur to me that my Brooks Brothers shirt and suits might be put together by people working in similar conditions. (They might not: for all I know Brooks Brothers has an impeccable employment record.) It literally never crossed my mind.

To be fair, I had several other stories to work on too, while I was in New York, and probably had to keep them apart in my mind to avoid getting muddled up. But the oversight looks rather shocking now. And it doesn't make me feel any better about the fact that I've never worn those suits.

The fact is that we have all learned to depend unthinkingly on other people, working out of sight and out of mind; and it's this combination of dependence and obliviousness that lies behind so many of the big problems facing us today. When we leave a light on, we don't think of the miners digging coal to fire the power station, and the carbon emissions they produce. When we put the rubbish out, we don't think of the vast acreage of landfill.

And we don't *want* to think about it: when somebody points it out, we find it irritating or painful, like a poke in the eye.

We call lamely for something to be done – but again, even here, we make ourselves dependent on others. We wait for the government to act, and when that fails to happen we feel disempowered: not only failing people like Lilia Luna and You Di Liao but also, as I hope to make perfectly clear, failing ourselves.

But there is another way! It's time to take control of our own destiny and change the world ourselves. And it's my belief that the business of clothing ourselves, second only to food and shelter, illustrates how we can do that as well as anything else.

chapter 3

Hoping to avoid the most boring parts of shopping, the author hires a "personal shopper"

But taking control of your destiny doesn't come easily. For as long as we can, we cling to the idea that others are better placed to fix things for us, either because they are more expert, or because they're cheaper – or both.

For instance: cuffs fray, jeans go thin at the knees and bum, jackets snag, leaving loose threads to dangle messily, and eventually your wife suggests it's time to buy myself some more clothes.

Well, mine does. And I do as I'm told, though – like many people – I hate shopping. As often as not the items I bring home from my sporadic retail adventures are deemed to be "not quite right". In some cases, if they're truly awful, apparently, and have to go back.

Since our daughter was born, my wife has enjoyed less time to oversee my clothing issues. Consequently I've found myself wearing tatty clothes far longer than I should.

Not very long ago, I had a lunch with a glamorous magazine editor, in a glamorous restaurant that had just opened, and set off from home in a jacket whose middle button had broken in half some weeks before. To hide that fault, I slipped the jacket off before joining her at the table – but admitting what I'd done after dessert I realised it was time to get help.

Which is how I found myself at a rendezvous with Nicola Robinson, London's foremost personal shopper, under the clock at Selfridges.

Through her company, Being Seen, Robinson advises up to 200 individual clients at a time on what clothes to buy, and where to buy them. This may sound simple, but Nicola seems to remember the design, colour and availability of clothes at more shops than I've even heard of. Thus, instead of getting a headache as I struggle to comprehend Selfridges's mighty sprawl, I can pad meekly behind Nicola and trust her to find whatever is needed. And I needn't worry that she's flogging me something unsuitable because she's not tied to any particular shop or designer.

Naturally, this service is not cheap. But for £1,500 a quarter, Being Seen members get up to six hours of chauffeur-driven consultancy, home visits from tailors, clothes delivered to work on approval, invitations to the launch of new collections, and access to celebrity hair stylists and make-up artists. More than a scruff like me would ever need, of course – but that's OK because Nicola also works for £50 an hour.

All she knows about me, when we first meet, is my size. That's enough for her to have put aside for me, in one of the store's peaceful suites, dozens of trousers and jackets, boxed shirts by big-name designers and a sizeable heap of sweaters.

But what next? Should I strip, while Nicola watches, like it's no big deal? Or pretend to be massively absorbed in each individual item, like a proper Being Seen client? I opt for the latter, and boldly pull out a sweater. Striving for the air of a connoisseur, I say I'd prefer not to wear anything in aubergine, and thrust the offending item into her hands.

That's fine, she says cheerfully. She doesn't want to force a "new look" on me, just get a clearer idea what I like. (At her office, she keeps a file on every client, with detailed notes about sizes and preferences.) And after I've outlined my clothing philosophy at greater length she goes off to find more.

Some of the items she's put out cost a fortune, but I guess there's no harm trying them. I slip on a pair of brown trousers by Nicole Farhi. Not bad, but not quite right. Then various jeans. Wearing a pair of Earnest Sewn, I try on a Prada shirt. It's black, which is not a colour I'd normally wear, but I like the slim cut. And on Nicola's return, I deliver my thoughts.

She agrees that Farhi's trousers aren't quite right. But she likes the jeans, urges me to take a Prada shirt in another colour, and asks which of three cord jackets, by Hackett, I prefer. (I opt for the brown one.) She also urges me to take a certain V-neck sweater by John Smedley.

We put everything aside and head together for Gap, just yards down Oxford Street. Here, Nicola whizzes round the shop piling clothes up in my arms: a brown cashmere sweater, a tweedy blazer and another with a blue stripe, a pair of brown cords, a dark grey shirt remarkably like the Prada, and a selection of T-shirts.

The total cost is £254. Then Nicola hurries me down South Molton Street towards Bond Street where she reckons I'll find an even more appealing V-neck at John Smedley's own shop than the one waiting for me at Selfridges. Alas, I don't, so we whiz back to Selfridges to pay for the goods already set aside. Here, the total cost is £569. I try not to look horrified and thank Nicola for all her help.

At home, after we've put our daughter to bed, Harriet requests a little catwalk show, and I comply. After seeing each item, she announces that it's all wonderful. Apart from the tweedy jacket ("a bit loud"). And the Gap shirt ("too trendy"). Oh, and the John Smedley jumper. But the rest, she says, I can keep.

I'm better dressed, perhaps, but not the slightest bit in control. Less so, perhaps, than ever.

chapter 4

Looking for a "story" but also genuinely intrigued, the author decides to sample every Christian denomination, to see which one might "fit". He starts with the Mormons

On Sunday mornings, at 9.50am, a complete stranger attempts to get my attention by ringing a bell belonging to the church at the back of my garden. For years, I ignored this tuneless summons to worship, placing a pillow over my head till it stopped – until my daughter came along, and lie-ins till nearly 10am became mere memories.

As an unbeliever, I never imagined that the bell-ringing was directed at me.

Nor did I pay attention when churches dropped leaflets through my door, or launched expensive advertising campaigns. Even promotions that generated media hoo-ha failed to score. Like many other people, I couldn't care less whether the church even existed.

I've not been confirmed, nor even baptised. I have attended church, occasionally, for weddings and funerals, but my understanding of the Bible stems from studying English literature – and from the feature-length dramas which used to appear on TV at Easter and Christmas.

I did flirt, briefly, with religion. It happened one rainy afternoon, when I was seven, after I'd watched some film about a nun. I climbed onto my bed, formed a steeple with my hands and asked God to supply me immediately with a new toy – or, failing that, some other outward sign of His existence. Nothing occurred. So I trotted off to ask my mother whether she believed in God.

Hemming and hawing, she seemed to indicate that, on balance, she didn't. And that was that.

But my lack of faith, though common, is untypical. Millions of British Christians regularly meet for worship – only a small proportion of the 39m who call themselves Christians, but still more than all professed Hindus, Jews, Muslims and Sikhs put together. Christianity remains strong: the queen is Supreme Governor of the Anglican church, and – in England and Scotland, at any rate – this fact confers on Christianity the status of established religion.

Churches have closed, it is true – becoming bars, restaurants and apartment blocks – but that process is two-way: elsewhere, congregations have built new churches, or adopted premises previously used as snooker halls, offices and even petrol stations.

So what have I missed? Hot stuff, presumably. Throughout history, people have been tortured – and murdered – for being Christians. And regular churchgoers still suffer persecution, in the form of mockery. To find out why they put up with that, I decided one August to give church-going a try, sampling denominations to see if any suited me. If I hadn't become a Christian by Christmas, I would give up; and maybe next year try some other religion.

I drew up a shortlist, each church with a Unique Selling Point, then photocopied a map of the UK to pick out branches at random. I might not always choose typical churches, or the best of their type, but by choosing randomly I hoped to replicate the experience of any other pilgrim.

*

On weekdays, Corey Chivers worked as a lawyer. But in his spare time he was bishop at the Church of Jesus Christ of Latter Day Saints (better known as the Mormons). One Thursday in September, I met Chivers at his office, and asked if his colleagues knew about his other life.

"People know I don't drink or smoke, so in that sense I stand out. Also, I never come into the office on a Sunday." Beyond this, even rank and file Mormons avoid extra-marital sex, and undertake to give one-tenth of their income to the church. They believe that

Christ reappeared in America – because that's what it says in the *Book of Mormon*, brought to light by the church's first prophet, Joseph Smith. When they are young, Mormon men undertake a two-year mission – largely self-financed – to spread the Gospels.

"We believe the Gospels will make you happy," Chivers said. "Everything around us is designed to make us selfish, and lie, and think of ourselves first – but we say, no!, I'm going to love my neighbour and look out for outcasts and the underprivileged. As you do that, you become extremely happy. Don't just take our word for it. Pray for it sincerely, after having studied. Literally get down on your knees and ask God to tell you this is right. We will have you converted by the end."

When Sunday came, I put on a suit – Chivers particularly recommended that – and drove nervously to the 1960s church on Exhibition Road. Crossing the threshold, I found myself shaking hands with a long series of smiling people who asked – usually in American accents – for my name, and where I came from. They also gave me a name badge.

In the crowded hall, the benches were luxuriously padded – which perhaps explains why nobody stood up to sing hymns. Nor did anybody move for communion. The body of Christ was brought to us in our seats: I took a piece, and popped it in my mouth. Nothing happened. Next came the blood… which turned out not to be wine, but water. (I took some anyway. Still nothing.)

Then began a part of the service which Chivers claimed to be unique: personal testimony from members of the church. "Usually it's very positive," he had warned. "But sometimes when I hear it I cringe, and wish I had a trap door." I could soon see what he meant: testimony, typically, consisted of children asserting love for parents, or vice versa – and also for Joseph Smith – before reciting the Mormon catchphrase, "I know the church is true." Charming to begin with, this soon became dull, and eventually mind-numbing.

There were exceptions. One man stepped forward to say, shockingly, that he'd received a letter informing him that his father, in Africa, had died. "At the moment I'm a sorrowful person," he stated, unnecessarily, "and I wanted to share this with you because I feel so much love". A young missionary broke into tears even before reaching the lectern. "I love the Scriptures," he sobbed. "The desire that you have to learn about the Gospel brings me great joy." (Despite this, he pulled a long face, and sniffed.) Another who burst into tears was a middle-aged woman: "I look at this congregation and feel I love you all. We have more than 50 nations here. I love you. I can't call you all by name but I love you!"

This was extremely awkward. I had not consciously radiated love towards these strangers: could they have misinterpreted the general mood, or was it just me?

After more than an hour, the testimony ended. Bishop Chivers, coming to find me, suggested a scripture class on the *Book of Mormon*, led by a woman with half-moon spectacles. "Can you see what a wonderful person you could be?" she said at one point. "These are not easy commandments to follow. To love someone who hates you takes a lot of practice…"

Before the class finished, Chivers conveyed me outside, for a tour of the church. Wherever he went, people slipped him envelopes – containing, presumably, tithed income in cash and cheques. On the stairs, a man shuffled up to Chivers, asking for an appointment to see him. Politely, the bishop introduced me to this man – a beneficiary of Mormon welfare programmes, he later explained – and reflexively I stuck out my hand. Only too late did I notice that he smelled strongly of poo. Retrospectively, I see that this was a perfect opportunity to love my neighbour – but for the next 90 minutes, until I found a washbasin, I could think only of the germs on my palm.

Next, Chivers led me upstairs, to a room where male members of the church – dressed in dark suits, like a convention of salesmen – had gathered for a "priesthood meeting". This, to my horror, comprised testimony even more banal than before: "I would like to talk about the welfare of my soul," said one American, typical of others. "I'm with one of the private equity shops in town. It's very stressful. I would have a hard time keeping balance were it not for the Gospels. I know the church is true."

To liven things up, I could have stood and announced that God doesn't exist. I didn't, because I had no wish to offend, and because I feared I might never escape. After three hours, I was parched; the low ceiling and bright lights were making me ill. I couldn't take much more.

Testimony seemed to confirm my worst preconceptions: that religion was boring and creepy. Karl Marx, memorably, likened religion to opium, but I wondered if it was more like cigarettes: an acquired taste, not especially pleasant to begin with. Alas, I've never possessed sufficient will-power to take up smoking.

chapter 5

Inspired by the example of big business, and an American magazine story, the author "outsources" the boring parts of everyday life to India

Having already put my shopping in the hands of a professional, then gone shopping for an organisation to look after my soul, I suppose my next move was predictable: I decided to outsource my life.

I wouldn't have done this if it wasn't for the American writer AJ Jacobs. If it wasn't for Jacobs, I would never have requested underpants from a married woman in Bangalore.

But Jacobs had inspired me. Unable to ignore the global trend for outsourcing business operations to India, he'd decided to outsource his life, and enjoyed what seemed like remarkable success.

Starting with routine tasks, such as ordering food and cinema tickets, Jacobs's agents in India moved on to increasingly delicate matters. They answered his e-mails, pestered his boss, and, on speakerphone, read bedtime stories to his son.

After he argued with his wife, he instructed one agent to resolve the matter online. "I can't tell you what a thrill I got. It's hard to get much more passive-aggressive than bickering with your wife via an e-mail from a subcontinent halfway round the world."

Something prompted me to try the same thing in Britain. After all, 60% of leading companies believe the service they get in India is as good as they could get here – and the cost is much lower. I get a dozen calls a day from good-natured Indians representing British companies.

Instead of resenting the outsourcing revolution I decided to embrace it.

The first company I approached, Brickwork, originally launched as a service for banks and other financial institutions. Vivek Kulkarni, its chairman and chief executive, previously worked in government and helped to attract many multinational businesses to Bangalore. For as little as $ 1,500 (£820) a month, he told me, I could have a full-time graduate assistant at my disposal for 40 hours a week.

Until now, I'd never have believed I could justify the expense of a full-time assistant. But Jacobs's experience suggests it might be worthwhile. He asked Brickwork to pester his editor about a magazine story idea he'd sent in. The letter his assistant wrote was insistent but polite. "It would be great if you could invest your time and patience on giving thought to (Jacobs's) plans. Do let him know ... Your decision would be accepted with utmost respect."

Jacobs loved it. "My boss can't just e-mail a terse 'No', as he might to me. Her finely crafted e-mail demands a polite response. The balance of power has shifted."

Brickwork had its limits, however; it declined to handle personal matters. So Jacobs hired Get Friday, a Bangalore-based service originally established to aid the thousands of Indians living abroad. (Most use it to run errands for aged parents back home.) The price for individuals is a reasonable $ 299 (£165) a month. And there's no limit to the number of requests you can make.

So far as I could tell, I was the first customer in the UK who isn't Indian. Sunder Prakasham, the chief operating officer, reassured me: "It really doesn't matter if the service is to be rendered in New York or Hong Kong or Bristol. Anything that can be handled through the internet or phone is manageable, provided the language is English."

The agent who contacted me from Get Friday turned out to be Asha Sarella, who had previously helped Jacobs. A graduate in electrical engineering and in spare moments an Indian classical dance teacher and salsa dancer, she had recently married and lived with her in-laws. There wasn't much work for electrical engineers in Bangalore, so she swapped to customer relations.

To begin, Asha had trouble understanding my British accent. "I'm sorry, Mr John. You speak a little fast. Can you repeat, please?"

But she got used to it pretty quickly. I sent her a lengthy list of tasks, all to be completed in 24 hours. Get me a table for two at the Ivy and tickets for the Test at the Oval. Book the venue for my daughter's birthday party, and hire the entertainer. Find a place where I can get a health check on Bupa (I haven't seen a doctor for a long time). Locate a Chloe "Paddington" handbag for my wife (absolutely the thing, at the time, apparently), and tell me the price. Find out where I can get cheap handmade shirts, and call Brooks Brothers in New York for a copy of the measurements I had done years ago.

Thinking I might have made it too easy, I asked her to call Marks & Spencer and get them to send me some new underpants. At the time, I confess, I thought this request rather amusing. I also asked her to find out if leading hairstylists in London and New York would take a look at my photo and advise on whether I might benefit from a new look.

Then I gave her the names and contact details for old friends I hadn't seen in a while, and asked her to get in touch with them, say I'd like to meet up. "Not quite sure if all the e-mail addresses are up to date," I told Asha. "Could you check?"

I wondered what I could do with the leisure time I would soon have. It occurred to me to take up the piano, perhaps write some poetry. I asked Asha to get prices for pianos and find teachers in my area. And I gave her the phone numbers of two well-known poets and asked her to get their recommendations on the best verse forms for an amateur poet trying to "take things up a level".

She offered no comment on the tasks – just asked when I would like my table at the Ivy. Four hours later, she sent a clutch of e-mails. The first politely declined to phone any poets without first doing some background research, and I hadn't allowed time for that. The next contained details of my nearest piano shop. She'd talked with the manager, who recommended an upright for beginners, costing £1,600. She also attached a list of piano teachers near me.

One detailed the closest Bupa health centre, complete with map. Another gave the name of seven leading hair salons, of which two were willing to take a look at my photo. But most impressive was the message she sent my friends. "Hi mates," it began. "It's been quite a while since we have met. Have been kept quite busy with my writings. But you know, I just hired a remote assistant all the way out in India to handle my tasks. And that should free a lot of my time.

"Now I intend to catch up with old friends like you. And do all the things I seem to be missing out on. I do miss you all a lot. It would be wonderful if we could meet up sometime soon. Individually or together, whichever works best. I hope this e-mail gets through. If not, I might need to ask my assistant to call each one of you." The message was signed "John-Paul", but beneath that was a postscript. "This is Asha, remote executive assistant to Mr John-Paul Flintoff, mailing you on his request."

I loved "Hi mates". And the PS made me feel extremely important indeed. I replied to Asha, thanking her very much. One of my friends soon replied: "I can't work out if you've been attacked by a virus or if this is for real. Either way, it would be good to meet up – when you get back from Bombay, perhaps?"

Less sensational was the news that she'd got me a table at the Ivy … in a few months time. Similarly, she reported disappointingly that demand for the Chloe handbag (£762!) was "crazy and unprecedented… the waiting period could run into weeks". Brooks Brothers no longer kept my measurements, and anyway wouldn't give them to a third party. And I would need to give Asha an upper limit so she could bid for Test match tickets on eBay. They were selling for £1,000 a pair.

And my amusing request for underpants? By mid-afternoon UK time, Asha had already worked a long day. She left me in the hands of a colleague, who sent a link to M&S underpants online. Arun pointed out that I'd need to choose between boxers, trunks and briefs, and indicate the size, colour and quantities I required.

I hated the pants on the website, but couldn't back out now. I replied (copying the message to Asha as requested) that I'd like an £8 pack of three Y-fronts, medium-sized, in a colour called teal. "Believe it or not, these are the pants I want," I wrote. "At least, they'll do. Usually I buy pants, and when my wife sees them she laughs for about an hour. Perhaps better stick to just one pack for now."

Despite this mild humiliation of my own making, outsourcing my life was proving a success. Work would continue overnight. As Jacobs put it: "I'm not wasting time while I drool on my pillow. Things are getting done."

But nobody in India can handle the problems that bother me most, those that need someone right here in my house, now. They can't tidy up my daughter's toys, move the radiator standing where I want the piano to go, or make me a cup of tea.

I needed to outsource locally, too.

So I tried Quintessentially, a concierge service I'd read about in upmarket style magazines. It claimed to offer access to the inaccessible – which in practice means upgrades, invitations to big social events and tables at the most fashionable restaurants. Surely Quintessentially could get me a table at the Ivy before December? It certainly should: a dedicated "lifestyle manager" costs £2,500 a year.

I left a message asking someone to call, but after two hours I'd heard nothing.

One does become accustomed, when one has remote executive assistants, to a swifter response. When the call did come through, I wasn't sure I liked the tone: I may have been softened by Asha's sweet voice, but this male caller sounded like a rather pushy estate agent.

I gave up on Quintessentially, having by now found a company called Buy:Time, whose "lifestyle managers" cost £25 an hour, with no membership fee.

Some clients book lifestyle managers at regular times each week, the founder, Claire Brynteson, told me. Others keep it ad hoc. Lifestyle managers do anything as long as it's legal: arrange parties, load iPods with music, shop around for better deals on a mortgage, collect dry cleaning and return unwanted items to shops, ferry domestic animals from London to Wiltshire, hire and supervise builders … The list goes on.

Feeling guilty going behind Asha's back, I asked Brynteson to find me a lifestyle manager at once. And soon afterwards I got a call from Sophie Appleton, asking what she could do for me.

To be honest, I was running out of tasks. But I asked her to collect a couple of pictures waiting for me at a Hampstead art gallery, and to fetch my favourite cheesecake from a nearby cake shop. Then, if she didn't mind awfully, I'd like her to find a plumber who could move that radiator.

Everything worked out fine, with one hitch. I hadn't made it clear that I only wanted a slice of cheesecake, and when Sophie phoned to check, I was asleep.

Consequently she arrived with a slab six times the size I needed. I did think about offering her a slice, but soon decided against it. Eating cheesecake is one thing I don't need to outsource.

chapter 6

The spiritual pilgrimage continues

On a Saturday night in Dundee's arts centre, David Robertson briefed me on the next step of my spiritual journey. We drank pints of lager, and Robertson, who called himself Dave – as in, "You might say to me, 'Dave, I can't come to service on Sunday'" – carried a mobile phone and a PalmPilot. Nothing in his appearance positively identified him as a minister of the Free Church of Scotland.

But he had strict rules. "We expect people to attend on Wednesday at 7.30pm, and on Sunday at 11.00am and 6.30pm. You have to make a commitment." Also: "You simply can't be a member of the church if you don't believe in God, or if you think the Bible is rubbish." (The Free Church accepts the Bible as the sole rule of faith and conduct.) "If you're open minded, I think you will be converted. You could go to your room tonight and have a visitation from an angel. Or you might hear something in church tomorrow."

The next morning, at St Peter's, I was handed a Bible and a book of psalms. The words were unfamiliar, but I managed to join the singing after a few lines – if quietly, because it felt dishonest praising a God I didn't believe in. After the sermon – readings from Luke, and thought-provoking analysis – the congregation rose and filed towards the linen-covered pews at the front for communion. Only if I had suddenly converted during the service – he warned me – should I step forward. Sitting alone at the back, I felt the exclusion of a dunce, or miscreant, and understood that peer-pressure alone might be enough to convert a weaker soul.

Afterwards, Dave invited me for lunch with his family, and some friends. After spoken grace – a novelty, for me – his wife,

Annabel, asked if I had many friends who go to church. I told her I didn't. "How strange!" she exclaimed.

A few weeks after leaving Dundee, Andrew Norris, the vicar in charge of three churches outside Taunton, in Somerset, invited me to his vicarage to observe a meeting with parishioners, to discuss baptism. I accepted, grateful for the opportunity to witness the discussion that precedes a more typical entry to religious life than my own.

Sharon and Ian – and baby Chloe – crowded the sofa while Norris, at his desk, put everybody at ease with his classically jolly Anglican manner. (Offering sugar with tea, he asked: "How many sins would you like?")

"In medieval times," he began, "it was considered awful if you weren't baptised, you were outside God's love. But I find it difficult to believe in that kind of God… It may be that you want to leave this for her to decide later. In this parish I've had children from five [years old] to 12 asking to be baptised, and that's really nice because they have a real motivation." A short-term alternative would be a blessing. (Norris's own children, as it happens, were not baptised till they were old enough to request it, but he doesn't mention that.)

Ian and Sharon have already made up their minds.

So Norris changes tack, explaining the ceremony's importance. "I hesitate to say that the church is like a club, because clubs can be quite exclusive, but if you are a member of the cricket club, and never turn up, then that is a bit meaningless…

"In the service you are asked, as it were, to agree that you believe in what the club stands for: God the Father, Jesus Christ and the Holy Spirit… I will make the sign of the cross and that is a bit like your membership badge. Then you're a soldier of Christ, so, er, go for it!" (Chloe gurgles.) "Well, I've sort of rabbited on, is there anything you'd like to ask?"

Ian, remembering his wedding, says: "Er, fees…?"

"No fees! There are no fees! This is about welcoming someone into the church, and God's love is not something you can buy."

Back at work, I received an email from David Robertson, in Dundee.

"I thought of you the other week," he wrote. "About four weeks ago, we had a young man walk in to the church. He is an engineer in a factory here. No church background – he just felt like coming. Anyway, after four weeks of attending he has now 'converted'."

This was encouraging, but it was becoming clear that I'd started my quest on a questionable basis. Travelling outside London involved little spiritual jeopardy: there'd never been much chance I would join a congregation in Dundee, or Somerset. I decided from now on to confine my search to London.

By this geographic measure, the Mormons remained in the frame. Their head of mission had invited me to observe missionaries at work. As a journalist, I saw this as a compelling assignment; but personally I felt nervous.

I decided to try a few other denominations first.

chapter 7

In which the author is troubled by rats invading his home, and gets in experts

---

Reading in my sitting room one night, after builders had left a hole in the kitchen floor, I heard a rustling. Had a pipe burst? Had someone broken in?

It was worse. Poking my head round the kitchen door I was greeted by two rats dancing a macabre reel and leaping at our food cupboards. They were not quite the size of cats but they were big.

One was a good eight inches long, and that was before taking account of its long greasy tail. And while mice would have vanished at the slightest human stirring, these boys looked as if they might stand their ground.

In the days that followed, I saw more. Then Harriet pointed out that her bank account gave her a free consultation from pest control professionals. I made a phone call and a man came round. He had sturdy boots and a branded T-shirt. I told him the rats were in the cellar. He tentatively pulled up one floorboard. I waited for him to squeeze through, but instead he put it back, went to fetch some packets of poison, and poured them hastily into the deep void. Then he went away.

Nothing changed. For days on end, we lay awake worrying that a rat was going to get into our young daughter's bedroom. It nagged at us every minute – especially when creatures chewed noisily at the floorboards beneath us.

One night, two of my traps went off. I went to investigate. One hadn't moved. Another had skittered across the kitchen, but remained empty. The third couldn't be found anywhere. I guessed that the rat, its neck broken by the trap, had fallen back under the kitchen floor.

I heard a scraping and crept out of sight. A rat stuck its head up, sniffed chocolate on the air and delicately thrust its nose into the waiting trap. I wasn't sure I wanted to watch it die, but kept my eyes on it and gasped as it pulled the chocolate from the trap without suffering any harm, then slithered back down the hole.

The following day, a dirty fug built up in the kitchen. It was coming from the hole. I was going to have to open the floor up and remove whatever I could find. I went across the road to get help from Brian, the bravest and most helpful person in our street. He brought a long hooked implement and dragged out the trap, with the stinking rat inside it. From its position, we calculated that the previous night's chocolate thief must have been standing on the body of this dead rat to carry out his daring raid. Classy animals, rats.

Chez Flintoff, we uphold the highest standards of hygiene. But in my area – unlike many around the country – the council continues to collect rubbish every week. So to find nosh rats hereabouts can't just lounge around the overflowing bins. Instead, they must break into houses.

I went around the perimeter of the kitchen filling in every crevice with wire wool, which rats don't like to chew on. Then I called in fitters to put down our beautiful new kitchen floor.

But the night after the boards were laid, as I sprawled on the sitting-room carpet watching TV with my wife, a shrill squeak announced that a rat was with us in the living room.

I emptied the room, piece by piece, and found nothing. I guessed that they were coming up through the holes around the radiator pipes, and repeated my wire wool trick. But psychologically they had us beaten: every few minutes or so we heard them scuttling among the rubble below, or chewing the boards.

(Rats, I have since learned, possess incisors that grow constantly. To keep the teeth short, they are obliged to gnaw through wood, lead, bricks, concrete and even steel.)

The kitchen floor was going to have to come up again. In fact the whole cellar needed opening up and sealing against any subsequent invasion – but who would possibly take on such an unpleasant, back-breaking job? Not my builder: he'd disappeared. The last time I saw him, he delivered a sermon about the importance of eliminating rats and even promised to call about helping carry out this sacred duty – but I've heard nothing since.

And what about Nancy? We don't want to make her scared of rats – she already has nightmares about butterflies and ladybirds. But on the other hand we don't want her to think that rats are lovely, and attempt to stroke them or share her food if one should suddenly appear before her. What should we tell her?

Not about Black Death, that's for sure. As every schoolchild learns, the disease – carried by the fleas on rats – appeared in Sicily in 1347, sweeping through Europe and killing nearly half the inhabitants in three years.

We think of it as a thing of the past – the last known outbreak in the UK was 300 years ago – but Yersinia pestis, as the bubonic plague is correctly termed, is still with us. More than 38,000 cases have been reported recently to the World Health Organisation by 25 different countries.

And the scariest thing is this: the plague has started to show signs of resistance to antibiotics. The French Pasteur Institute reported that plague can pick up this resistance from all-too common bacteria such as salmonella and e-coli – posing "a global threat to public health".

Of course, rats don't only carry plague. Two out of three carry cryptosporidium (a cause of gastroenteritis); only slightly less common are salmonella, listeria (which causes septicaemia), toxoplasmosis (blindness), Q fever, Hantaan fever, and the lethal Weil's disease.

A female is capable of producing ten-strong litters, ten times a year. Recent estimates put the UK rat-count at between 60 and 100 million. After successive mild winters and warm summers, rats have become fitter and stronger. They've thrived as rubbish collection has become less frequent.

Another big issue is sewers, where water companies do little to eliminate rats. In most areas, barely a fifth of sewers are inspected as a matter of course. The rest are checked only if something goes wrong. It's not unknown for retired engineers to be called out in emergencies and asked where pipes run.

Similarly catastrophic is the decision by 67 per cent of local authorities to cut back on rodent officers. Where I live, pest control was closed in 2004, and only re-opened after complaints from residents. But the service came back at a cost to users, and that seems to put people off: take-up fell by 75 per cent, despite reported sightings of rats going up nearly 50 per cent.

According to the National Pest Technicians Association, the result of councils charging for pest-control – and people declining to pay – is an increase of 69 per cent in the rat population over seven years. "Councils should not charge you to deal with rats," says the NTPA's John Davison.

As it happens, nobody was answering the phone when I called pest control. So I went out to buy poison from a hardware shop.

A recent study involving the British Pest Control Association indicates a new generation of "super rats", able to consume previously lethal doses of two of the four most common types of second-generation anti-coagulants. But my own rats showed an admirably old-fashioned tendency to kick the bucket after scoffing the bait.

Less happily, they chose to die under my floorboards, releasing released a dire smell that lingered in the throat and made me want to heave. Other rats found the smell less off-putting. Indeed, they daintily cannibalised the corpses – taking great bites from them – and in doing so poisoned themselves.

(An additional, no less cheerful spin-off of infestation by rat, I have discovered, is the incidence of bluebottles, which lay their eggs in the rotting rodent before circling my head as I work at my computer upstairs.)

Clearly, killing the rats wasn't enough. I had to stop them coming into the house in the first place. I returned to the hardware shop and bought a device that uses ultrasound – beyond the hearing of humans, cats and dogs – to irritate the rodents. But alas, my rats didn't seem bothered.

I succumbed to the inevitable: I called Rentokil, which promised to keep poisoning the rats and removing the bodies till they stopped coming – then seal up any entry holes. (Do it the other way round, they warned, and the trapped rats will chew their way out.)

The fee was vast, but I signed up all the same, and Rentokil duly sent along one of its best technicians, Paul Boggia.

He did what I hadn't done: leapt into the murky, malodorous cavity beneath the floorboards with something like the joy of a child entering a paddling pool, noted "signs of activity" and removed two stiff rats ("Out you come, Roland!").

To say that I enjoy Paul's visits would be an overstatement – I don't relish removing 159 screws from the kitchen's plywood floor, and replacing them all again afterwards – but I've learned a lot from his brisk approach.

I can't wait till he brings along a colleague with a camera that inspects drains for cracks from the inside. And I'll be delighted when Paul finally declares that the last of the rats has died and that we can seal up the walls and install Rodent Radar – a Rentokil-branded device that captures and gasses rats with CO_2, then sends you an email or text message advising you to be rid of it.

In that event, assuming that I've not succumbed to Black Death, it will give me great pleasure to wrap the deceased rodent inside a couple of plastic bags, and lob it in the bin.

chapter 8

*After working as a rubbish collector,
the author visits a landfill site*

When you're wearing rubber gloves, a streaming nose is no joke.
To begin with, I wiped it on the sleeve of my new reflective jacket.
But after ten minutes of hauling dustbins, I'd covered the sleeve in
muck; so I reached inside for my sweatshirt – bearing the logo of
Sita, the company that collects rubbish in the Royal Borough of
Kensington and Chelsea – and wiped my nose on that.

The job of dustman is not fun, and nor is it improved by rain.
From every bin-bag, water poured down my leg and into my steel-
toe-capped boots. Meanwhile the rain continued to fall, dribbling
down my neck and inside my jacket. After half an hour, even my
underpants were soaked.

On Royal Crescent, a wet dustbin slipped from my shoulder.
There was only one way to steady it: with my head. So that's what
I used. After emptying the bin into the noisy dustcart, I wiped
a sleeve against my ear to remove a dark smear of goo. Coffee
grounds? I hoped so.

In the royal borough, every household got two collections a
week. The streets I was doing, spread between Holland Park
Avenue and the Westway, boasted some of the most prosperous
homes in the country, and my guess is that they produced are no
less rubbish than the national average – a tonne a year, for a family
household.

I was working with the crew of K2, one of 17 dustcarts covering
Kensington. Cliff, the team leader, had thinning hair and a heavily
lined face. Steve had bulging eyes and wore a beanie hat marked
"England". The third loader, Tim, was younger and inexplicably

cheerful. Then there was the driver, Mick, whose short bursts behind the wheel did not exempt him from the arduous business of throwing rubbish into the grinding jaws of his machine.

We left the depot at 6.20am. Theoretically, our shift ended at 4pm. But dustmen are not paid well – even team leaders earn just £15,000 – so to finish as quickly as possible we foreswore breaks and gathered rubbish like men possessed. Steve, for instance, generally carried eight bags at once.

Kensington and Chelsea has invested heavily in its fleet. K2, which cost £150,000, had two compartments at the back: a large one for ordinary rubbish and a smaller one for recyclable paper, glass and plastic. For residents, this provided an excellent opportunity to Do The Right Thing.

The vast majority didn't bother. Some didn't even use bin bags – they just threw everything loose in the bin – so Cliff, Steve and Tim had to carry heavy loads up slippery basement stairs then back down again (with bags, just one trip is necessary). Other people did use bags, but without bothering to tie them, so the contents fell out.

In a basement on Lansdowne Crescent, a flimsy white bag spilled its contents over my feet. Cursing silently, I put down the other bags I was carrying and gathered up the unappealing leftovers: pasta coils, eggshells, soft tomatoes, a scattering of sweetcorn and upturned boxes oozing creamy sauce.

That wasn't even the worst thing you find in bin-bags. Squinting through the rain, Cliff held up a piece of glass. "The ****s that put loose glass in the bin: they're the worst." Not long before, a loose shard sliced through the muscle behind his knee, and Cliff had to be taken to hospital.

There were other hazards too. On Holland Park Avenue, Cliff pointed to a house and said: "Leave that one – there's rats."

A few houses along, somebody had put out 30 beer bottles in a cardboard box. Soaked by the rain, the box collapsed when I picked it up, so we carried off slippery bottles by the fistful. Inevitably, two or three slipped, scattering brown glass across the pavement.

But the funny thing was, nobody seemed to notice. People looked right through us, as if dustmen were invisible. The hurtful truth, I found, was that the public does not esteem dustmen. Which is odd, because the British are tremendously productive of rubbish. With a few far-seeing exceptions we're unthinking chuckers-away, infinitely messier than the French or the Germans, let alone the Swiss. And without dustmen we'd be in big trouble.

At 1.30pm, our shift came to an end. Ceremonially, we threw our gloves into the rubbish in the back. Then we drove to a transfer station in Wandsworth, beside the Thames, where we paused on a weighbridge behind a cart from the neighbouring borough, Hammersmith and Fulham, then reversed towards a vast hatch and evacuated our load. On the way out, the cart was weighed again, and an illuminated screen gave us an adjusted figure. Cliff did his sums. Over seven hours, we'd collected 10.8 tonnes of general rubbish and 2.4 tonnes of recycling. "Not bad," he said, "for a Monday."

In waste management, demand is entirely driven by legislation – without laws, we'd probably still throw rubbish from our windows – and every new law makes the industry bigger.

Of course, it's not just about collecting rubbish. Most companies are also involved in what happens next. There are three options. Some is recycled (we'll get to that later). A fair bit is burned, to produce energy: a plant in the Midlands takes municipal waste and converts it to power for the car factory next-door. But incineration, though admirable, is not enough. What do you do with all the ashes?

The vast majority of rubbish is used as landfill. Nine London boroughs use the transfer station in Wandsworth to send waste by river, saving as many as 100,000 HGV movements which would otherwise clutter our roads. The company which operated this station, and the tug boats and barges, was Cory Environmental, which ships hundreds of thousands of tonnes of rubbish to the landfill site it runs in a place called – would you believe it – Mucking, in Essex. As the next stage in my odyssey of filth, I caught a ride on one of Cory's tugs.

In the past, before rubbish was containerised, it lay in open barges, loosely covered in tarpaulin. The man at the wheel this morning, Malcolm, remembered decks crawling with maggots –

and MPs retreating indoors to escape the stench as barges passed by parliament. "Nowadays," he shouted, as 1,400 horsepower engines boiled up the river beneath us, "we don't hardly know what we're carrying."

All the same, as we drew alongside the seat of government, and – soon after – the London Eye, the City and the Dome, I became dreadfully self-conscious. We no longer stinked, perhaps, but we were hardly silent, and certainly spoiled the view. But perhaps this is a good thing, because just as passers-by screen dustmen from their consciousness, so, ordinarily, we're unaware of the fate – and sheer quantity – of the stuff we chuck in our bins. Just possibly, the sight and sound of these barges might help to address that indifference.

And what happens next? Where does rubbish meet its doom? I travelled onwards, to a converted quarry outside Ipswich. Consisting of 10m cubic metres of void space, Masons landfill took in 300,000 tonnes a year. At this rate, the facility – owned by Viridor – should last another 20 years.

The site is divided into cells – of about 200m square – just as a farm is divided into fields, explained Bruce Mackie, the manager. Each cell, lined with plastic like some vast garden pond, costs around £1m to engineer. "You build a cell," Mackie added, "and when that's three-quarters full you start the next one."

To show what he meant, Mackie took me for a spin in his jeep. We parked beside a sign marked "Cliff Edge, Stay Away". On one side, there was a 40m drop. On the other, the last of the day's dustcarts drove over a similar depth of compacted rubbish to evacuate their loads.

Ordinarily, a low-slung dustcart would not be considered ideal for this kind of off-road activity. But Mackie's rubbish is not loose. He uses compactors – monstrous juggernauts on spiked wheels, worth £750,000 each – to press three times as much rubbish into the void as would be possible without them. "We pack it tightly," he said, "because we get more money that way. When you get yourself a hole, you want it to last." And driving on top of tightly packed rubbish – even at a depth of 40m – does not pose a great problem for the 150-or-so dustcarts which arrive each day.

"I love rubbish," Mackie announced, suddenly rhapsodic. "It always changes. It never ceases to amaze me what people throw away. Some people will throw away a CD player because the fuse has gone… Once, we had 20 tons of Polo mints – that made the place smell nice for a few days." Another time, he received a consignment of liquor, confiscated at Felixstowe. More recently, there was some ham: "Fifteen tons of tinned ham. Nothing wrong with it, but it was shipped too late. The customer – a supermarket – insisted on six months' shelf life. It arrived too late. They didn't want it."

When the heap approaches the point we were standing on, it's capped with a further layer of plastic. "It's like a pie. The plastic is the pastry, and the rubbish is the meat." On top of that comes 2m of earth, which allows the area to be used for pasture. Also built into this pie is an elaborate system of pipes. Some pump methane, which is burned to produce electricity. The others suck up leachate, a murky distillation of landfill juice that collects inside each pie like noxious gravy. "Savage stuff. It's black, with floating solids in it. Imagine what you'd get if you dissolved a can of catfood in warm water. Imagine the nappies, batteries and leftover aspirin," he added with evident relish. "It stinks, like nothing you've ever known. Only a very few people get to smell it. When they do…" – to illustrate this fearsome eventuality, Mackie waved his arms wildly, then pretended to stuff a hanky in his mouth.

Understandably, people do not clamour for landfill sites near their home. "People say it has a horrible smell, but I say it's the smell of money."

Mackie – wouldn't you know it – believes his site has proved itself a good neighbour. "The regulations are second to none," he said. "Landfill sites can be shut down almost immediately. And that happens. The inspectors might come and say there's too much dust, or noise, or smell – or too many gulls." For each of these problems, Mackie had a solution. Dust is eliminated by sprinkling water over the entire site. Gulls are kept away by falconer. To discourage other scavengers, fresh waste is covered up each night with earth – which is also heaped up to deflect noise. Around the perimeter fence, Viridor had planted oak, hawthorn, alder, birch and willow to conceal the site from houses below. And in a far corner, Mackie installed what looked like five-a-side football goals. A sports facility for local youth? No, they weren't goals after all, but nets for catching rubbish blown by the prevailing wind. "People live 300 yards from the site," Mackie declared, "but if you mention the landfill, most of them say, 'What landfill?'"

We climbed back into the jeep and drove to an adjacent field, studded with standpipes. Reaching down to one of these, Mackie turned a valve and I was astonished by the force of the gas whooshing out. "You could power a town the size of Exeter with the amount we produce."

There's more than just landfill to Mackie's operation. He also runs a recycling plant, producing about 30,000 tonnes of recycled material each year. When I was there, the workers were sorting plastic sheets. In a cabin at the top of some stairs, three men flourishing knives pulled coloured material off a conveyor belt, leaving only the clear stuff. The coloured material – mostly blue, but some of it black – was dropped through a hole in the floor, to be gathered by a fork-lift truck and packed into bales. Further down the line, the clear plastic is sorted into different sizes, and then impurities – rubber bands, scraps of paper – were picked out. But here and there the plastic was covered in stickers, and it was simply not economical for Mackie's staff to remove those. Packed into bales, the plastic sheets were destined for China, where extremely reasonable labour costs turned them into grade one material through the removal of these stickers by bored individuals armed with scissors.

There's little demand for the end-product: roadbuilders some-times use glass beneath the tarmac – but there aren't enough roads being built to take it all. Similarly, the price of recycled paper has dropped dramatically; and the more we recycle, the faster the price falls.

At the Environmental Services Association – like leachate, biosolids and practically everything else in this business, the waste industry's trade association has a name which conceals more than it reveals – the chief executive, Dirk Hazell, strikes a note of cau-tion. "You have to be careful not to regard recycling as always the best thing to do. People think recycling does not cost anything.

But there is a cost. For example, the cost of putting lorries on the road: it's not very good environmental practice to drive 35 miles to recycle a glass bottle."

Outside his recycling unit – where some quixotic individual has planted flowerbeds – Mackie leads me to a rainbow spectrum of baled recyclables. To the left, grey paper. Next, coloured plastic – known in the trade as "jazz' – consisting largely of bottles of fabric conditioner, Harpic and Sunny Delight. Beyond that, whiteish plastic bales which sometimes explode when traces of milk inside them produce gas. Finally, on the far right, we come to mixed metals. "This is the one that stinks in the summer," says Mackie, fondly tearing a label from a can of dogfood. "A real fly's disco."

From here, the cans are sent away to be separated into steel, aluminium and tin at a specialist plant; one of just a few dotted across the country. Among others, there's a plant in Dorset where different types of plastic on a conveyor belt are scanned by a machine and blown into the appropriate container by air-jet. Outside Manchester, there's a unit that recycles fluorescent lighting and sodium lamps – separating glass, metals and highly poisonous mercury.

These specialist facilities are not cheap to build. To pay their way, they must attract rubbish from near and far – including, possibly, abroad. "But if you say to politicians, 'we have the technology, we want to import waste'," says Hazel, "they say you can't do that. It's a political decision."

This is the nub of the problem: Sentiment versus Money. We approve of recycling in principal, but don't want to spend extra on it, and we don't want foreign stuff. The government pays lip service to the concept – issues ambitious targets – and local authorities lay on special collections. But market forces aren't impressed. Market forces think recycling is a load of rubbish.

"Next time you get a chance," says Bruce Mackie, "take a look at a box of Mr Kipling's jam tarts. There's the most enormous amount of packaging. Why do they do that? Because that's what customers want? Because of food regulations? No, it's to stand out on the shelves."

A bottle of fabric conditioner, Mackie says, will last a thousand years. "Why can't you take that back to the supermarket to refill it? You could walk into a supermarket with almost as much as you take away. And you would, if you were penalised for throwing things away."

The only way to reduce waste, he says, is to charge for collections according by weight. "If your bin had a barcode on it, and it was weighed on the dustcart, you'd get an accurate bill. Then you'd turn round to Sainsbury or Tesco and say 'I don't want all this packaging'."

I'm not convinced. Most people, I suspect, would dump rubbish in their neighbours' bins, just as they currently dump the big stuff in somebody else's skip. But I'm touched that Mackie should bother to devise this waste reduction strategy.

After all, this is a man whose livelihood depends on an endless supply of rubbish.

chapter 9

The author visits a local seamstress, and considers whether he might be able to do some of his wife's clothes adjustments himself, saving considerable sums

---

Lovely woman, Galina. She's from Russia, has a sing-song voice with a pronounced Russian accent, though she's lived in England, so far as I can tell, for decades. Her husband, whom I've never met, came from Africa to study in the Soviet Union. One of their sons is a successful ballet dancer, and I've met him several times as I drop into the family HQ with an item of clothing for Galina, a seamstress, to adjust.

Virtually every clothes shop in our part of north London recommends Galina to customers who need to get things taken in or up, or let out. Harriet has been using Galina's help for more than a decade. In my visits to her workplace, which is actually her flat, I've met people I knew, and even a couple of women well known from their appearances on TV. Whenever I arrive, Galina gives a cheery welcome, perhaps comments on my appearance – usually asserting that I've lost weight. Once, she tried to get me interested in her adherence to the Hari Krishna movement. I listened politely but avoided getting drawn in. It may be very good, but I'm not ready to embrace something so exotic. There seems to be something wilfully eccentric or anyway rootless about people who embrace a religion from half-way round the world.

Of course, Galina is from half-way round the world herself. So that's fair enough. Anyway, I remain hugely affectionate towards her, and can't imagine anybody failing to feel the same way.

But I have become increasingly frustrated by my dependence

on other people to do the simplest things. This was brought home most dramatically by a visit to Galina with Nancy, then little more than a toddler, to get some elastic sewn into her new ballet shoes.

I watched one of Galina's assistants do the work in front of me, for £5. It couldn't have been easier.

In future, I vowed, I would do all but the most complicated tasks myself.

After all, I had plenty of sewing lessons at school. These actually started at primary school, where I made a rudimentary pin-cushion out of felt and scrunched up tights. (My mother still has this.) But in my last year at primary school my otherwise wonderful teacher took it into her head that she was going to teach the girls to make skirts. This project lasted several weeks, and went against my already rather pronounced sense of social justice: we boys had been given nothing to do, and that didn't seem fair. So I went on strike, and with another boy actually skipped off one afternoon to the local shops. Alas, I was obliged to return at closing time to collect my younger brother, whereupon I was seized by the deputy head (male, as it happens) and roundly told off.

It only occurs to me now that this injustice might explain my rather uncommitted attitude in the textile classes that were obligatory for one term each year at my secondary school. I did, it's true, make a couple of things that satisfied me: a sponge bag for toiletries taken on school trips, and a person-shaped cushion in the likeness of the Labour politician, Tony Benn. (I don't absolutely know why I chose to make Benn's effigy, but remember that my father had favoured him as a candidate for deputy leader of the Labour party at around that time.)

More often, I misbehaved rather badly. With a boy called Jeremy I leaped about on the tables wearing a mocked-up headband, shouting "You cannot be serious, man!" in impersonation of the fiery Wimbledon contender John McEnroe (textile classes, that year, presumably took place in the summer term).

It would never have occurred to me at school that, despite my considerable indifference and hostility, the teachers were managing to transmit skills and even a positive enthusiasm for sewing that would come back to me many years later.

Certainly, there seemed to be little connection, then, between the textiles lessons and the clothing I wore. Indeed, the very idea of wearing home-made clothing would have filled me with horror: what would my classmates say? I didn't do spectacularly well even with shop-bought clothes: my parents could never be induced to spend the barmy sums necessary to keep up with what my peers deemed appropriate. As a result, I was not infrequently accused of wearing "bogus" items. I remember particularly an Argyle-type sweater from Marks & Spencer that a much younger boy enjoyed jeering at ("Bogus Pringle!") as well as a pair of white tennis plimsolls with green trim ("Bogus Green Flash!")

The awareness that people might judge my clothes to be deficient does to some degree remain with me, but it's more complicated now. I like dressing up occasionally – swaggering about in black tie, for instance; or getting out for winter the wonderfully preserved 30- or 40-year-old overcoat, in bright orange Harris Tweed, from Harrods, no less, that once belonged to my wife's great-uncle Max and was given to me by his widow, great-aunt Peggy, some years before I married Harriet; in fact, while I was still only her boyfriend from university.

That said, I also take a pleasure that I can't entirely explain from looking scruffy, or anyway from continuing to wear items that are past their best. I can't entirely explain either of these quite contrary joys, but hope that I may one day find out.

chapter 10

Soul for sale (still)

At St Etheldreda's, a Catholic church in Holborn, Father Kit Cunningham met me in his office before lunchtime mass, and immediately began talking about Original Sin. The Mormons had been oppressively upbeat; this, to me, was going too far the other way. How about accentuating the positive? "We're flawed creatures, born with a propensity to sin," he said. "A lot of people do not accept the church because it's a reproach to their lifestyle."

Unprompted, Cunningham launched several attacks on his competitors, particularly the CofE. "Anglicans have no moral theology," he said. "Anything goes. The Ten Commandments, you can take them or leave them…" When I told him I'd visited the Mormons, and taken communion with them, he rolled his eyes. "Well, you can't take Communion here, because you're not a member of the church."

I'm impressed that people give up their lunchtimes for mass. Don't they feel they're missing out? "No. They've spent the time well. One woman told me she used to waste the whole hour looking in shop windows."

We talk about confession, which Cunningham represents as, essentially, a cheap alternative to psychiatry, and prayer. "You start with vocal prayers, Our Father and Hail Mary, and this raises the mind to God. You can raise your mind to God at any time, for example when you are waiting for a train. Just think of Him: it can be a mind-blowing operation. Cultivating a sense of the presence of God is very useful."

Does Cunningham think I might convert, one day? "I would think that you will succumb, eventually. This is where the grace of God comes in. It will trigger something in you. Tell me, the genius of Shakespeare and Beethoven – do you think that can go out like a candle? What is the difference between a corpse and a human being?"

Inside the church, amid beautiful stained glass and life-sized statues of saints, I tried to think of an answer. In all, 23 people arrived for lunchtime mass. Even the last, rushing to their seats, paused to genuflect towards the altar. I couldn't do that without feeling foolish, so I didn't even try. But that omission, in turn, seemed foolish – and the same applied when congregants kneeled to pray, crossed themselves, or uttered verbal responses. I had learned that fitting into a church requires familiarity not only with doctrine, but also with procedures: the slogans, the dance-steps.

It was time to change my approach once more. A journey which had begun as an idea for a magazine story had gradually turned into something more personal. (Much of the "work", after all, needed doing in my own time, on Sundays.) I decided to abandon my self-protective guise as journalist – to stop asserting, in effect, that I was here only because of my job. For my next visit, I would turn up unannounced, and leave my notebook at home.

Additionally, I resolved to try something far removed from energetic evangelism. By early November, I had conceived the self-regarding idea that – like Groucho Marx, unwilling to join any club that would accept him as a member – I could never join a church that showed interest in me, only one that was virtually indifferent.

But that particular notion was easily exploded. When I telephoned the Greek Orthodox church nearest my home to find out about services, the man who answered said gruffly that Sunday service lasted three hours. Was that the best service, I asked, for a first-timer? "You can come along if you want. No one will stop you," he said, and put his phone down. His bluntness, admirable in some respects, did not attract me. If the Greek Orthodox weren't interested in my soul, I wasn't interested in them. I struck them off my list.

But the Quakers seemed pleased to hear from me. The Society of Friends, to use their proper name, have no formal doctrine, or sacraments. They base their outlook on the Gospels, but acknowledge debts to other religions, and even to people of no declared religion. Most peculiar of all, they have no clergy, and they worship in silence – no hymns, or set prayers – interrupted only when an individual (any individual) feels moved to speak or pray.

At the Meeting House in Hampstead, the seats were arranged in concentric circles, around a small table. For once, there could be no hiding at the back. I wondered how to react if somebody opposite should stare at me: do I smile, stare back blankly, or get up and run away? The solution was to gaze intensely at a gap between two table legs, causing peripheral vision to blur.

Over the course of an hour, the thoughts that passed through my mind consisted principally of work, family, and death. There were four interruptions. The first speakers, both women, stood to ask for prayers to help absent friends. A man with shoulder-length grey hair rose to announce that prayer is "like surrender", and to offer a parable involving diseased wood, highly prized by carpenters for its spotted appearance. Finally, after about 55 minutes, a woman in the centre circle stood to give, essentially, a response to the previous comments. "What is God?" she asked. "Well, he's certainly not a magician, to do magic at our request. So who do we 'surrender' to?"

When the meeting ended – marked by an outbreak of hand-shaking – newcomers were invited to introduce themselves; and over coffee, several individuals asked me how I liked the meeting. To one, I said truthfully that I'd enjoyed it, and would happily come again – but that I didn't believe in God. His answer surprised me: "Oh, well, that doesn't necessarily matter."

At last, I was making progress. My enthusiasm revived. The following Sunday, woken as ever by the bell, I dressed at speed and walked round the block. By chance, my first attendance at All Saints fell on All Saints day – and this was also the day on which the Church of England unveiled its new Order of Service. Instead of delivering a sermon, the vicar stood in the pulpit explaining the changes. He flourished a succession of prayer books from throughout the ages – ending with the photocopied order of service that had been folded inside our hymn books.

The words to be spoken by congregants were printed in bold type. There were only a few changes: instead of praising Christ in the third person, for instance, worshippers should now say: "Praise to you, O Christ". "This is to bring us closer to Him," the vicar explained.

But at another amended passage, he said the new wording was "of no consequence at all". My first response to this stereotypical Anglican vagueness was to smile, but on consideration I thought – so why bother? If set prayers aren't to be taken seriously, how can they possibly raise the mind to God (as Father Cunningham had indicated they should)? Worse, the droning recitative provided just enough distraction to prevent the mental focus I'd achieved among the silent Quakers.

chapter 11

How a man named Danny Wallace started something beautiful on a whim, making the author's similarly whimsical religious pilgrimage seem rather hollow

The Victory Christian Centre is a Pentecostal church, less than a mile from my home in north London. Whenever I passed it, going to and from work, the pavement outside overflowed with worshippers who looked uncommonly cheerful.

I no longer feared walking into churches, but this one I approached with trepidation. As a tall white man I was certain to stick out in a congregation that was overwhelmingly Afro-Caribbean. By now I'd started to suspect that people join churches that suit their social class, intellect, and cultural background. Believers, predictably, disagreed; insisting that only one church – their own – was the right one; but I clung to my view. So what was I doing here? Was this visit tendentious – like the trips to Dundee and Somerset, merely a stab at something exotic? I hoped not.

In the packed foyer, I was welcomed by a woman in a splendidly coloured suit, with a badge identifying her as usher. "Er, this is my first visit…" I said. She beamed, and walked me into a windowless hall, steamy with breath from the previous service. Every seat was taken, so she pointed me towards the balcony, and another usher directed me to a seat at the front.

A young woman slipped in beside me, introducing herself as Michelle. She'd attended since May, she said, having been saved in January. (From what? I almost asked.) Admitting I was a first-timer, I asked what I should do. "You just praise and worship."

How? She pointed to the stage, where a dot-matrix board hung on the wall. "You see that? Just follow the words."

The noise, when the service started, was astounding. One woman led the prayers, supported by a full band and eight glossy backing singers, with microphones. My plan had been to join in wholeheartedly. And despite the offputting presence of video cameras, that's what I did. (Except at the end, when the Pastor induced congregants to open their cheque books: I hadn't thought to bring mine.) As well as singing at full voice, I clapped to the rhythm and swayed from side to side. And when Michelle raised her hands – palms up, in the Pentecostal fashion, as if to catch a beach ball – I did the same. I even fluttered my fingertips, like Al Jolson. But was I worshipping, or just going through the motions?

My religious pilgrimage, though sincere, had started on a whim, and mere intellectual curiosity. Was that enough? I might have concluded that it wasn't – but then I met Danny Wallace, whose own whim had turned into the most extraordinary success.

Wallace established a movement that brought happiness to hundreds of thousands of people worldwide. Tony Blair, hearing about this, sent him a message of support, followed by Prince Charles. Not long before I met him, Wallace was invited to launch the International Philanthropy Workshop, in partnership with New York's Rockefeller Foundation and the German Bertelsmann Foundation. Eight powerful billionaires – whose identity must remain hidden – sat quietly as he outlined his ideas.

Wallace started his mass-movement, one lazy day in 2002, without any idea what it was for. He placed a free ad in a London newspaper saying "Join Me". Respondents had only to send a passport-sized photo. Then they would be "joinees". "Christ, I was bored," he admits.

The first person to respond to the ad was Christian Jones, of London NW1, who kindly sent with his passport photo the menu from his local Indian takeaway, the Madras Valley, and recommended the chicken dansak. Then several more people wrote in, and Wallace soon possessed more passport-sized photographs of his followers – previously complete strangers – than Jesus had disciples. (Not every response was positive. One, written in crayon, comprised the single word "wanker".) When I met him he had nearly 9,000 joinees. In his flat in Bow, an entire wall was covered by passport photos: putting these up, Wallace told me, caused him to develop a particularly painful case of "Blu-Tack thumb".

His original, rather hazy idea was to collect 100 followers then stop. But these weren't just passport photos. They were human beings. As more and more joined him Wallace started to feel responsible for them. He worried when they got restless, urgently asking him (through his rudimentary website, joinme.co.uk) what exactly they had joined for. When one, Joinee Whitby, set up a fancy site of his own (joinee.co.uk) Wallace feared he might lose control of the movement. He decided to provide them with a purpose.

But what should it be? Initially he contemplated using his followers for mischief: sending them, for instance, to buy every ticket for the first night of the next Ben Elton musical and walk out as the curtain went up.

Hardly less whimsical, he decided instead to send out a commandment that joinees "make an old man happy". Eager to do his bidding, they hit the streets to carry out ad hoc good deeds for male pensioners, and sent back photographic proof. But a joinee in France wondered why old women were not included. Soon Wallace was commanding that his followers commit random acts of kindness on people of either sex – and any age – every Friday.

One of his previous big ideas was premised on a "booze-fuelled" bet with his flatmate, the comedian Dave Gorman. As a result the pair travelled round the world tracking down and photographing anybody they could find with the name Dave Gorman. It took six months, resulted in a book and a TV programme – but was regarded by Wallace's girlfriend, Hanne, as typical of his "stupid-boy projects". She left him, returning only after he promised not to do anything like it again.

Thus, when Join Me was in its earliest stages, he told her nothing. And he still said nothing as the project spun out of his control. But one day Hanne discovered in his flat evidence of what was going on. (Wallace was abroad at the time, promoting Join

Me on Belgium's leading chat show.) This time she left him for good, though she remains friendly.

Others have essentially agreed with Hanne about Join Me. "The Observer said this was a pointless book by a pointless man. But that's what a lot of people like about it."

In the years since he started Join Me, Camden's Madras Valley takeaway has become a site of pilgrimage, routinely cleaned out of chicken dansak by Wallace's disciples. His website, souped up, now offers tips to joinees in nine languages. And Wallace has published a follow-up: *Random Acts of Kindness* contains hundreds of sweet ideas, many suggested by joinees, including: "Run ahead of a street cleaner and pick up some rubbish for them", "Say something nice about someone behind their back", "Pop a sugar cube next to an ants' nest", "Wish good luck to all you pass outside the local Youth Court", and "Text someone goodnight".

When people start doing acts of kindness, he says, they tend to be small ones. "And they can blame it on Join Me. It's an excuse, it stops them feeling embarrassed. But then it becomes second nature and they realise that when they do something nice that makes them feel good, too."

Has Join Me changed him? "I'm not sure that I have become more spiritual," he says tentatively. "I don't believe in God, as such, but I believe there is good in everyone." After pausing for a moment he says: "I wasn't particularly cynical before I did this. Cynicism is overdone. It's joyless. But this has pushed me into a more optimistic outlook.

"Sometimes I get overwhelmed by it all. But not because of me. I don't think of this as something I did, it's something that happened to me."

chapter 12

On the streets with the Mormon missionaries

My Christmas deadline, by now, was getting close. I hadn't tried as many denominations as originally planned, but the ones I did try were diverse: variously with or without clergy, hymns, musical accompaniment, fine clothes, incense, a broad ethnic and social mix, and transubstantiation. In short, I'd sampled a greater range of Christian experience than many practising believers. But if I hadn't deliberately sought out Christianity, how might Christianity have found me? It was time to get in touch with the Mormons, and spend time with some missionaries.

From morning till night, Elder Tholl, 20, from Utah, and Elder Verral, 24, from Wales, walked the streets and rode public transport trying to strike up conversations. They were almost constantly rebuffed. People usually turn away when they identify themselves as members of the Church of Jesus Christ of Latter Day Saints. "Around about the 'Jee-' of 'Jesus'," Tholl said (though I suspect it may be as early as the "Chu-" in "Church"). Even when they make appointments to visit people, they frequently find that the person they've come to visit, presumably having forgotten about the appointment, is not presently home. But they didn't seem the least bit sorry for themselves.

On the bus from Hyde Park, Tholl started a conversation with a man reading the Racing Post. "Is this the right way to Westbourne Park?" "Yes." "Is that where you're going?" "A bit further." "Do you live around here?" Initially the man looked irritated, but Tholl, who has an engaging manner, brought him round. Nevertheless, the conversation ended prematurely when we arrived at our bus stop.

Our destination was a modern block of flats, where a Colombian woman was waiting to learn more about the church. Rather than introduce me as a journalist, the Elders decided, they would describe me to her as "a friend". And that's what they did, shortly before launching into their sales pitch.

Tholl, the American, spoke first. He asked compassionately about Matilda's sick husband, and gushed as he spoke of the love he feels for his own family. Then he suggested some New Testament passages for Matilda to read, in halting English, and with a few simple questions he brought her to agree that these passages prove that God exists.

Among other issues addressed in the 90-minute meeting was a lesson in how to pray, following a formula prescribed in Tholl's flip chart. And while Tholl flicked through illustrations at the front of the *Book of Mormon* – showing Jesus making his appearance in the American continent – Verrall explained how the *Book of Mormon* was brought to light by Joseph Smith. Then Matilda read a passage from that controversial testament, and once again the Elders asked her what she thought it all means.

In response to their questions, Matilda frequently addressed her unvarnished conjecture towards me, perhaps because I was the oldest of her three visitors. In describing me as a friend, the Elders had failed to make it plain that I was not one of them. And Matilda didn't seem to notice that, unlike them, I had brought no Bible. So I nodded, and smiled – but for the whole 90 minutes I said nothing.

At the end, having scheduled a further meeting for next week, Tholl suggested a closing prayer, and asked Matilda to decide who should say it. She pondered a moment, looked from one to the other of us. Then she said: "I'd like him to say it," and pointed a finger at me.

chapter 13

A depressing chapter

You might be wondering, by now, how this religious pilgrimage is connected to making clothes. Well, I'm going to have to ask you to be patient. My journey from mindless consumer to maker of my own clothes was gradual.

It was prompted, as often as not, by me looking for things to write about, and finding that the things I read, and the people I met, transformed the way I looked at the world.

I started the religious pilgrimage in the hope that it might make a good "story". It might amuse or impress an editor. And I found out about "peak oil" the same way.

Oil is not everybody's preferred topic of small talk. It tends to make the eyes glaze over. But the consequences of a terminal shortage are horrific, and should worry us all.

Without plentiful cheap oil, motor and air transport become unviable. Our financial system, premised on endless growth, is incapable of addressing new, shrinking economic conditions. And when you remove artificial fertilizers made from fossil fuels, the earth can support only 1bn or so people – so we seem to be heading for mass starvation.

I first learned about this on the internet, but have since read books and watched documentaries, variously sensational and sober. One, A Crude Awakening, comprises straight interviews with economists, geologists, professors of physics and politics, and a former acting secretary general of OPEC. But the impact is profoundly shocking.

One interviewee, Matthew Savinar, is asked if we face something like the challenge President Kennedy presented in the early 1960s – to get a man on the moon in ten years. "The problem we're facing is more like colonising Pluto," Savinar replies. "If JFK said we're going to have a hundred thousand people living in three-bed houses on Pluto in ten years, then obviously we would not have been able to accomplish it."

A physics professor at Stanford is asked, "Are my grandchildren ever going to fly in an aeroplane?" A gripping question, he replies. "And I think the answer is probably no."

The film grimly demolishes the case for many wished-for alternatives to fossil fuels.

To replace today's 10 terawatts of fossil-derived energy with nuclear power would require 10,000 of the biggest nuclear installations and the world stocks of uranium 235 would be exhausted in less than two decades.

Hydrogen is unlikely to develop because users won't invest in it till there's an infrastructure, and the infrastructure won't be built if users aren't there.

Biomass is inefficient: it takes more energy from fossil fuels to create ethanol than you get out at the end. And if the entire world's available land were given over to producing ethanol to supply just the 1.5 billion people living in rich countries, it would still only meet 15% of current consumption.

Wind and solar are intermittent and unlikely ever to produce the amounts we enjoy now.

Economic consequences of peak oil promise to be severe. Richard Douthwaite, of the Foundation for the Economics of Stability, says our debt-based financial system needs replacing fast, before it collapses as loans become unrepayable.

"Our particular money-creation system – in which banks lend money into existence on the expectation of growth – is like a pair of spectacles which give short term economic issues such prominence that they obscure our vision of the future. So it is hard to get sufficient political momentum to make sharp, uncomfortable changes to counter the slow-growing, high-impact threats we are facing, such as climate change, loss of fertile soil, dropping water tables, shrinking biodiversity and human population growth.

"It is imperative that we use our remaining fossil fuels as capital rather than income, investing it in projects which rapidly increase our renewable energy capacity. At the same time, we have to gradually redesign our settlements, retrofit our buildings, transform our agriculture, and contain our population in order to substantially reduce total energy demand. These objectives cannot be achieved in conditions of resource wars, famine and insecurity."

The director of A Crude Awakening, Basil Gelpke, is a TV news reporter by background who assures me that as a journalist he comes across a lot of "good stories" and is not easily impressed. "Also, I'm not really a Green person. I'm rather conservative and I like our way of life." But after reading about Peak Oil in a paper from an Australian hedge fund, he felt compelled to find out more. After all, he has two children. "I felt there was a terrible threat out there. I went through the usual stages of being depressed by it and nobody wanting to listen to me."

I felt the same when I first tried telling Harriet, who worked at the time for a fashion magazine. I talked about how certain elements of the world she lived in might not be available for all that much longer. She got cross, said she didn't like the sound of the future I was describing and ended the discussion – though she's since put up with many more along the same lines.

When I tried telling a friend, a strenuously committed environmentalist, he replied: "To be honest I think this is a red herring. We are nowhere near peak oil – as the current unseemly scramble for Arctic mineral wealth shows. Climate change will kick in way before peak oil. Sorry."

He's since changed his mind, but just as climate change attracts furious denials, so does peak oil. The most common argument is this: that higher oil prices will make it more affordable to drill less accessible deposits, so there's no problem after all. But that overlooks an important point: oil isn't like other commodities. At some point it will take more than a barrel of oil's worth of energy to drill for a barrel of oil, so the job won't be worth doing however high the oil price.

Is that moment coming soon?

In 2004, BP's Lord Browne proclaimed, "We have to demonstrate that there has been no shortage of oil, and that there is no shortage of oil, and that there never need be a shortage... there is no reason why there should be any shortfall in the foreseeable future."

But in the same year, Shell's then chairman, Sir Philip Watts, told investors the company had over estimated reserves by 20 per cent. Internal emails were requisitioned by lawyers which made it clear the chairman and others had known about the problem for some time and deliberately lied about it. They face criminal prosecution in the US.

Since then, the former oil industry geologist Jeremy Leggett has shown in his book, Half Gone, that the annual BP Statistical Review of World Energy relies substantially on third-party material; and states, in small print, that the figures shown do not necessarily meet US Securities and Exchange Commission definitions and guidelines for determining proved reserves. "They don't even believe the figures they are publishing!" writes Leggett. "And this is an energy bible used by researchers the world over."

As for Opec countries, Leggett points out that the size of their stated reserves has remained the same each year for a decade – indicating that the amount they have discovered each year has precisely matched the amount they produced over that period. You don't need a PhD in maths to think this extraordinarily implausible.

The known facts are these: the amount of oil discovered each year has been shrinking for four decades. The last time we discovered more oil than we consumed was 25 years ago; today, for every barrel we discover annually, we consume three. Production is already in terminal decline in 60 of the world's 98 oil-producing countries, maybe more.

The world's two largest oilfields, which once contained more than 80bn barrels each, were discovered in 1938 and 1948. Since then, discoveries have been tiny by comparison, and rare. In 2000 there were 16 discoveries of 500m barrels or bigger. In 2001 there were nine. In 2002 there were just two and in 2003 there were none.

Who would drill in the Arctic if oil was abundant elsewhere?

When I first heard of peak oil, in 2005, I wondered why the government was doing nothing to raise the issue. Colin Campbell, co-founder of the Association for the Study of Peak Oil, offers an answer: "There is little hope of politicians taking the lead. It's much easier for them to react to crisis when it happens."

All the same, after watching A Crude Awakening two years later I decided to phone the Bank of England, the Treasury, various government departments, the CBI, the Association of British Insurers and oil companies to ask if they had any policies in place to deal with Peak Oil.

The answer, in several instances: "How do you spell that?"

The Treasury referred me to the Department for Business, Enterprise and Regulatory Reform ("This is not a treasury matter.") DEBERR said it predicts no problems "for the foreseeable future". Ultimately, a spokesman said, the world may never run out of oil because "new forms of energy may come through to fuel transportation and so on". (He didn't elaborate.) The Bank of England politely explained that they have no policy. The CBI mused that the issue fell between its economics team and another covering business and the environment. The ABI sent me a report it had commissioned on the long-term global impacts of climate change: this didn't mention the word "oil" anywhere.

One oil company was willing to talk to me but only on a totally off-the-record basis. This nervous precaution is telling, particularly since what I was told was freely available on the internet.

But a BP spokesman scoffed: "Why should we have a policy on Peak Oil? Peak Oil is just a brand, a consultancy, a bunch of academics going round making money selling books and talking at conferences."

I didn't find this convincing, but to be sure I decided to find out how much money the retired geologists and economists and others in the Association for the Study of Peak Oil are paid. I learned that one of the best known individuals recently accepted just £200 for a speech. Is that a lot? Brendan Barns, of the leading public speaking agency Speakers for Business, says £200 would not cover most people's travel expenses. "It's a paltry amount. What would you get from any professional, a lawyer or an accountant, for £200? Nothing. For BP to say they're doing this for the money is laughable."

BP, by contrast, makes billions of pounds in profits each year. It's not hard to see which side has the greater financial stake in this argument.

Agriculture as practiced by mainstream farmers uses 10 calories from fossil fuels, as fertiliser and in transport costs, to produce a single calorie in food. Without oil and gas, how can we possibly keep up food supplies? Already worldwide grain production, per head, has started to fall. And bio fuels are encroaching on valuable crop land.

A report commissioned by the US Department of Energy and published without fanfare – in effect, buried – in 2005, warned: "The problem of the peaking of world conventional oil production is unlike any yet faced by modern industrial society. Without massive mitigation more than a decade before the fact, the problem will be pervasive and will not be temporary. Previous energy transitions (wood to coal and coal to oil) were gradual and evolutionary; oil peaking will be abrupt and revolutionary."

On the net, increasing numbers of people have started to upload survival plans, which on first reading strike an almost comically bleak note. But on second and third reading many of their prognostications seem reasonable and logical.

On one, headed Twilight of the Modern World, the author advises: "The important thing to remember is that our present society will not continue for much longer. Some trades such as plumbing and mechanics will be useful now and in the future. But lawyers will be (even more) useless when law and order breaks down."

The world is full of jobs like a shop cashier which do not pay much and afford no useful skills, he adds. People in such jobs should save as much money as they can and spend time in libraries learning about mechanics, first aid, self-defence, sailing, horse riding, fishing, plumbing and carpentry.

Additionally they should start insulating their homes, growing their own food, and stocking up on essentials. ("Think how much candles will cost when the power cuts begin.")

Peak oil and climate change are two sides of the same coin. One is about what comes out of your exhaust, the other concerns the stuff you pump into your tank. A shortage of the latter, I suspect, will energise more ordinary people to take action than an excess of the former. Mercifully, solutions to one usually help to fix the other – so long as we don't all rush to replace oil by burning coal, which is horribly polluting.

"Peak oil leaves us with no option but to move to a more sustainable, renewable-energy-fuelled economy," says Douthwaite. "Getting there requires taking a running jump over a yawning chasm. There are no stepping stones. The world on the other side will be very different. Radical changes are required. Making small improvements to a failing system, rather than revamping it entirely, just will not work."

Some people think that nothing will work. One is Gregory Greene, director of another peak oil documentary, The End of Suburbia. "It looks as if we are pretty, ah, fucked," he said in a recent interview.

Campbell, the godfather of peak oil and founder of Aspo, is less certain. "We are facing some kind of unprecedented, unparalleled situation," he says, "and that explains why it is so difficult to accept it. We identify a species called Hydrocarbon Man: his days are definitely numbered. Whether mankind, or homo sapiens as a species, will carry on living some different, simple way – that's another question."

chapter 14

Hoping to "save the world", the author throws himself into mainstream politics

I was standing outside Brighton Pier, on my soap box, in the biting wind. People were hurrying past, eager to take advantage of the first break in the heavy rain: young families, school girls, a crowd of Sikhs. Most studiously ignored me. Others offered a nervous smile and hurry past.

I'd never made a political speech before, but stood up straight, waved my arms a bit and called out: "Hello! Can I have a moment of your time? I'm not selling anything, I don't want your money. I just want two minutes to talk to you ..."

Before I continue, I should explain where I started my political odyssey. In 1987, my father stood for parliament in Plymouth. He attracted substantially more Labour support than previously; but failed to oust the politician who had done so much to split the anti-Tory vote. In other words, I grew up sympathetic to the Labour party and fiercely averse to its opponents. But times change, and a few years ago I decided to join the Tories.

Why? Because the New Labour government was a terrible disappointment. I marched against war in Iraq, but they disregarded my call for peace. As for climate change, and peak oil: I've switched to eco light-bulbs, a green energy supplier, an electric car, and a doorstep delivery of local, seasonal food. I also put my name down for an allotment. But the government seemed unwilling to take the steps scientists tell us are necessary.

Joining the Tories had started as a joke – a way to shock my right-on friends. But there was something serious about it too. Britain's political system restricts an individual's participation to just one vote every five years or so – a vote that can be used by the winning party to justify more or less anything. By joining a party with a realistic chance of winning elections I thought I might help to shape its policies.

Throwing myself into the project with enthusiasm, I attended all kinds of events, even including the annual gala dinner of the Gay Conservative Association. I didn't mention that I am married with a daughter – but then I also didn't mention that when I was at school I helped to collect money for striking coal miners. Unsurprisingly, my plot failed. I didn't belong. By the general election my party membership had lapsed. I avoided voting altogether by going on holiday.

There always have been people disillusioned by formal politics, but there seem to be more of us today than ever before. Look at the decline in voting. Labour won the election in 2005 with 9.5m votes; in 1992, Labour got 11.5m votes – and lost. Meanwhile, party membership has plummeted: the three main parties, in 2001, had a quarter as many members as in 1964. Rather than chase new members, their leaders seemed to have developed a hunger for cash donations from plutocrats.

Political analysts say my withdrawal from politics is typical of people my age and younger. In the past, young people started voting around the time they started to pay taxes. Today, young people don't seem to be picking up the habit, and old party loyalties have eroded. Few people nowadays want to identify themselves with a political party by putting posters in their windows; in the 1950s, to do so was utterly normal.

Not so long ago, an independent enquiry delivered a devastating critique of the state of formal democracy in Britain. Political parties and elections have been "a growing turn-off for years", it said. But the cause is not apathy: single-issue pressure groups are thriving, some 20m people regularly volunteer, and hundreds of thousands have joined protest marches. "The problem," the report concluded, "is that we don't feel we have real influence over the decisions made in our name."

The advent of a new Conservative leader, was – well, mildly interesting. I was impressed by what David Cameron did to raise the importance of climate change, and stirred too by his sympathetic social commentary, summarized by cynics as "hug a hoodie". But was this merely the same manoeuvring Labour had previously effected: stealing the clothes of your opponent in areas where your own party is weak, while simultaneously throwing a handful of policies at your core vote in appeasement?

Frustrated and confused, I rejoined the… Labour Party. I joined specifically to support John McDonnell's bid for the party leadership – or at any rate to oppose Gordon Brown's coronation, which didn't seem an absolutely brilliant idea to me at the time, though I daresay that Brown may be a wonderful chap. I confess that I'd not heard of McDonnell, a left-wing MP, till a few weeks earlier, but I admired him for daring to stand, and for setting out his policies clearly.

In hope of a cure for my democratic malaise, I took the train to Brighton and Hove: Britain's newest city hailed me no less urgently than Wigan previously summoned George Orwell, when he set out to understand the working class. Me, I was looking for trendy lefties – people a bit like myself, relatively well off and given to earnest hand-wringing. People who might have answers to the big political questions. Who should we believe? Is voting a waste of time? Does it matter that you can't tell a Tory from a Green (or can you)? Do we have the politicians we deserve?

As the national capital of right-on, earnest progressives, London-on-Sea (as the city's commonly known) is a stronghold of the Green Party. But it's not exclusively the preserve of radicals. One of its parliamentary seats, Hove & Portslade, was gained by New Labour in 1997 and remains a key target for the Tories.

By tradition, Hove is characterized as genteel and elderly. But Hove has a disproportionate number of people living in bedsits, as well as youngish professionals like me. Analysts have catchy names for these demographic types: Grey Perspectives, Bedsit Beneficiaries and Urban Intelligence. Many would be inclined towards New Labour, and would have voted for Blair in 1997. They're key to the outcome of the next election, not just here but nationally.

Arriving in town on my fold-up bicycle, naturally I went first to Hove's health-food shops and alternative-therapy centres – Planet

Janet on Church Road, and the nearby Sanctuary Café. Here I met a group of vegetarian teachers, no less disillusioned with Labour than me. Matt McKee and his partner Gwyneth Curtis are the parents of eight-month-old Kai; they'd moved here from inner-London for his sake. McKee works as a science teacher in a secondary school. Their friend Kate Heym teaches in a primary school.

Try as I might, I couldn't excite them about formal politics, only personal ethics. Over nut roast, gurgling from small children, and dainty folk music from the café's speakers, Heym remembered turning vegetarian as a teenager under the influence of a teacher. "We had a sociology teacher who talked about what it meant, what the animals go through…"

Children can exert an influence on teachers too, she said. "In our school, we're finding it difficult to get the council to give us recycling bins for paper, which is prehistoric, and I thought at first, can I really be bothered to take it all myself? In the end I had to. It was the kids who decided it. Putting a piece of paper in the dustbin would be like swigging a bottle of whisky in front of them."

I was grateful for the reminder that political change can be effected at the personal level. ("More is done by being a positive example than by being a whingeing git," says McKee.) But I wasn't sure that setting an example is enough.

*

Joanne Heard joined the Conservative party two years ago. She's been a supporter ever since her mother correctly predicted that an incoming Tory administration would give her a scholarship for private education. She's standing for the council at next year's elections, and took me for a drink at the local Conservative club, a smoky place with noisy music and slot machines. "Not many young people," she noted glumly as we walked in.

She has an instinct for public service. She's run a Neighbourhood Watch scheme, and she's putting on a show to raise money for Alzheimer's. But she only became evangelical about formal politics after a friend was elected as a councillor in Crawley on the toss of coin. "It was 500 votes each. They had to flip a coin. On the basis of that, Crawley council switched from Labour to Conservative. So every vote counts."

Heard believes party loyalty remains essentially tribal. But her partner is a Labour supporter. Why is that? "He knows what Maggie Thatcher did in the north," she said darkly. "He watches a lot of documentaries, delves into things."

The next day, a Saturday, I found Heard among the Conservatives working on a stall in George Street. With balloons and leaflets they urged people to sign a petition against "Brown's cuts to the National Health Service."

Wasn't it a bit cheeky, Tories fighting to protect a Labour invention? Not at all, said Brian Oxley, leader of the Tories on the council. "It's a settled debate. People want the NHS to be there for their family and to work as well as it can. David Cameron said recently that founding the NHS was one of the great achievements of the 20th century.

"This is an important issue. The system is stretched already, and now people are going to have to drive here from Worthing for Accident and Emergency. I would like to see the people responsible for these cuts trying to get here by car on a bank holiday!"

Mike Long, who chairs the local Conservative association, said it's a good thing the main parties all occupy the middle ground. "That's where Britain wants to be. We don't want to be far left or far right. These days politics is about who can manage things best. It's like Marks & Spencer. UK Plc will work better under a change of management."

So the difference is merely competence and commitment? Like Heard, Oxley has a strong public-service ethos. "The city has always had Labour administrations but I still get things done for people. I think that politics can be a noble cause. That sounds ever so – well, I don't know, naïve, but you do have to have some idealism."

I was impressed by how many people rushed to sign the petition. Most were elderly, and identify themselves as Tories by inclination. One, Phil Cooper, said he's supported Labour and the unions but had had enough of the tax rises, and the war in Iraq.

Several passing toddlers seemed keen to take a balloon, but their parents looked aghast. One woman did let her grandson take a specimen of inflatable propaganda, and only when it had been tied to his coat did I hear her say, "Oh, is it political? I can't see anything without my glasses." Another agreed to sign the petition but said firmly that she would continue voting Green.

One man wheeling a bike refused to take a leaflet. I pointed out that it only asks him to oppose cuts to the NHS. "They're Tories," he said, as if that settled everything. He refused to give me his name. "Call me 'Man with Bike'."

I told him what I was doing, about being politically agonized and so on. He sighed. "Look, there is nobody I can vote for at the moment. Iraq has made me most disillusioned. And climate change needs to be tackled. They're building another lane on the M1. It's going to cost billions. Are they going to tax aviation fuel? I don't think this will be tackled till something terrible happens." Something like Hurricane Katrina? "Yeah, when Brighton turns into Venice they'll do something."

I asked Oxley why people are cynical about Cameron. Will he disappoint us just as Blair has done? "No, because he is starting things from first principles. There is a genuine debate. He's trying to make the party a reflection of the country as a whole."

But Cameron's innovations haven't all gone down well with party members. The Tories in Hove & Portslade rejected candidates from Cameron's A List in favour of a local man.

Mike Weatherley, the prospective parliamentary candidate, was among the people handing out leaflets this morning. I asked if he's bothered about climate change as well as the NHS. "It was Mrs T who started off the environment debate. She highlighted global warming before any other politician. I'm really glad that David Cameron has taken that on board. It needed someone like him to do it. Of course policing and anti-social behaviour are important, but if we have not got an environment in 100 years those things will be meaningless."

After 90 minutes, the defenders of the NHS packed up early. They'd run out of space for signatures. As they wandered off, a dilapidated man approached me with a slavish smile. "Excuse me, sir… are you the new Conservative candidate?" I didn't know whether to be insulted or pleased.

A little distance away, I found that the Tory campaigning had an unforeseen political impact. A fundraiser from Friends of the Earth was talking to a woman with a pushchair and a young child who held one of the Tory balloons. "I think in some ways it was the balloon that made me stop and talk to you," she told him. "Because Cameron does talk a bit of sense about the environment."

At the council offices, I mentioned this to the leader of the Greens, the grizzled but bustling Keith Taylor. I asked if he welcomes the Tories' environmentalism. He doesn't. "Cameron is just testing the water. Anyway, the Tories continue to support the extension of runways at Gatwick."

*

A longstanding Labour member and union man, Jon Rogers, agreed to meet me in a pub, the Charles Napier. On arrival, I was greeted by a man lowering his trousers and mooning at friends inside. Mercifully, this was not him.

Rogers is much given to old-fashioned socialist talk about the working class. Won't that put people off? "The working class is almost everyone, in my book. I wear a suit to work so you could call me middle class, but I sell my working power and that makes me working class."

But he's affable, and funnier than this makes him sound: he made me laugh aloud when he talked about getting "quality time" with his family on demonstrations. He's also surprisingly optimistic, considering how little confidence he has in his own party's leadership.

How did he account for the decline in political participation?

People are passionate about their civic responsibility, he said. Look at the march against war in Iraq, the Make Poverty History movement, and the increasing numbers of demonstrations against cuts in the NHS. But we're losing faith in political parties, he believes, because they offer little choice. "They ought to express coherently different philosophies on what they stand for. If there is no choice, then what was the point of the Chartists and the Suffragettes fighting for the vote?"

At Labour's annual conference, controversial issues such as the party leadership and the replacement of Trident are deliberately smothered. "The conference has been decaffeinated. We have over-learned the lessons of the 1980s, and we're going to have to unpick the damage that was done when nearly everyone thought that Blair walked on water."

As Rogers sees it, the Tories aren't necessarily the biggest threat. "The problem with my family is that most of them vote Green. The debate within the family is between people like me who say, why should we abandon our own party, and the others who say we're wasting our time, we need to build an alternative."

Better to be inside pissing out, I suggested, than outside pissing in? "I'd rather be inside, pissing in."

Fundamental to this approach is the idea of "managing your MP". "You write to them every so often, and you put up a motion in your branch. That can provide cover for them in the whip's office – an excuse for not voting with the government. And even if they think you're a pain in the arse, they won't be openly rude because you're one of the people going out to campaign for them at the election. We have dozens of members in our branch, but only half a dozen come to meetings. If you get involved you can have disproportionate influence. That is one of the side-effects of the decline in activism."

According to the Power Inquiry, one of the greatest causes of political disaffection is the sense that we have no power at all between elections. What Rogers suggested might help overcome that. But do I really need to join a party? My own local councillors, in London, are Lib Dem, my council is run by Tories, and my MP is Labour. Thanks to Tom Steinberg, a policy wonk who formerly worked at the Prime Minister's strategy unit, and his techie colleagues at MySociety.org, I can manage them all at once. MySociety's websites enable anybody easily to identify representatives at every level, to see what they're doing, and correspond with them at the click of the mouse.

I called Steinberg. To be absolutely clear, he said he's not interested in getting people to polling stations. "But in between elections," he said, "there are more than a thousand days and any number of decisions are taken every day. We have tools to help you influence those decisions."

*

Before leaving Brighton and Hove I wandered to a rally about climate change put on by the Labour MP, Celia Barlow. With sponsorship from a big local employer, Barlow had got hold of a film projector so that voters could watch Al Gore's documentary, *An Inconvenient Truth*. "I have seen this before," she told the audience, largely comprised of Urban Intelligence and Grey Perspectives, who overflowed the seats and stood all round the hall. "I was shocked and horrified... Remember the tsunami? The danger that we face now is far larger. This is a moral issue we are facing."

The first speaker was a professor at Sussex University. In keeping with the revivalist tone of the meeting, he said he used to be sceptical about climate change – but no more. "It has become very clear that there are going to be some big impacts." And that's what his slide show made clear. Most chilling were the warnings about what might happen if the Amazon dies off, or Greenland melts – both already happening. These "tipping points" might lead to catastrophic climate change beyond human control. "The last time the temperature was just three degrees hotter, the sea level was 25 metres higher than today."

Among other speakers is local teenager Jordan Stephens, one of nine children from across the country appointed to be "ambassadors" for climate change – making talks at schools and so on. He was impressively confident, and obviously on top of his brief, but on this occasion his feisty challenge to the audience – "How many of you have ever bought a long-life bulb?" – fell slightly flat as everybody immediately put a hand up.

Barlow was parliamentary private secretary to the then-minister of state for climate change, Ian Pearson, whom she had invited along to talk. His speech began defensively: "I want to tell you what we are doing, and then you are going to tell me that we are not doing enough. And I agree with you."

But he made clear that the government will not be able to do more about climate change without overwhelming pressure from citizens. "The more people press the government to do things, the more government will do."

Taking him at his word, I grabbed the minister afterwards. Conscious of what Man With Bike told me, I asked furiously whether Pearson was doing anything to persuade the Department of Transport not to spend £1bn on widening the M1. How will road-building reduce emissions? "I have not been involved on the M1. But congestion is a problem too."

And remembering what Rogers said about Trident being taboo at Labour's conference, I asked if the £25bn wouldn't be better spent on clean energy. The minister shook his head. "We need a deterrent," he said.

I returned to the hall, where an elderly resident lamented the seeming impossibility of recycling plastic. She said it broke her heart to put milk containers in the bin.

A speaker from the Friends of the Earth, Martyn Williams, told the audience about an experiment on Newsnight, in which a reporter spent six months trying to tackle his own emissions. "He managed to cut them by 35 per cent, by doing fairly simple things. That's great, but it's really difficult for him to do more. The rest is down to government. For instance, it's very difficult for any of us as individuals to do anything about coal fired power plants."

It doesn't matter what party you belong to or vote for, Williams added, you must use your politicians properly. "Don't just vote and leave them unbothered for five years between elections. The problem will not be solved by this prime minister or this secretary of state. The problem is going to last for 50 years. Cutting emissions by 60 per cent by 2050 is a NIMTO target – Not In My Term of Office. We need annual targets, so we can hold governments to account." The fact that there is going to be a climate change bill in the Queen's Speech, he said, was entirely down to pressure groups. "Over recent months 600 MPs have been visited in their surgery by Friends of the Earth supporters."

It was a valuable lesson, and confirmed what others had already taught me. Indeed, I'd learned something from nearly everyone I've met on the road to Brighton Pier.

The person who had the most impact was Rogers, the card-carrying champion of the working class. Others may have matched his public spirit, or his analytical reach – and shared his misgivings about Gordon Brown, which soon became very widespread indeed – but Rogers combined those with a palpable sense of excitement and optimism.

And yet… Rogers is just one man. He's not the official voice of Labour. So I can't say I've reached a firm conclusion about which (if either) of the two main parties I should support. In fact, the presence of the similarly enthusiastic Taylor, and others, on the council proved that voting Green needn't be a wasted vote. So yes: I've learned all over again that voting really can be effective.

But more important, I think, is the duty to do more as a citizen in a democracy. And that's pretty well what I tell the 50 or so baffled people who kindly gather round my soap-box – an unforeseen but strangely unavoidable destination on my political pilgrimage – to listen to my impromptu speech-making.

I talk about the urgency of the many issues that need addressing, and remind them that it may be four years till the next election gives them a chance to register their wishes. "Don't wait!" I yell. "Use your politicians properly! Use them now!" Then I spell out carefully the name of websites, founded by Steinberg, that might help. "TheyWorkForYou.com allows you to keep track of your MP's activities!" I howl into the onshore wind. "And WriteToThem.com helps you to, er, write to them!"

It's not the finest political speech in history, but nobody heckles. A man from Croatia, having just acquired British citizenship, seems genuinely impressed. And a group of schoolgirls take turns to shake my hand because I have heard of their home-town, Harpenden. The rest smile, step back, and stride onto the pier.

chapter 15

*The author meets a Green Goddess who can't
give up smoking*

When the man from Friends of the Earth announced, "It's very difficult for any of us as individuals to do anything about coal fired power plants", I believed him. I frequently repeated it to other people. I joined Friends of the Earth, hoping this would help to pile pressure on the government.

It took me a long time to realise that we can do a great deal indeed as individuals, about this and many other things. For instance, we can stop buying electricity from companies that use coal to generate it. If we all line up as customers for wind power, there will be no market for coal. End of problem.

But that assumes that everybody will do the same as us. In practice, what are we to do about other people, who keep doing the "wrong" thing?

A few years ago, I came across a fantastic story about a woman who gave out spoof parking tickets to people driving their children to school in 4x4s. I got hold of a few tickets myself and subsequently met their designer, Sian Berry, by then a leader of the Green Party.

I was interested to notice that she rolled her own cigarettes. She started on one just as we were leaving the health-food emporium where we chatted for an hour or more. And perhaps because it takes so much longer to roll a cigarette than to smoke one ready-made, she still hadn't finished it by the time we reached the offices of the glossy magazine for which I was interviewing her. She stopped outside, looked for somewhere to drop it, then stepped in to choose from a selection of clothes selected for her to wear in the photo shoot.

Pushing the various garments aside, Berry said flatly but cheerfully that she refuses to wear anything red. Why? "Because I'm a Green". That said, she immediately afterwards declines a shirt in a particular shade of yellow: "It will make my hair look green," she explains. There's Green, it seems, and green.

Quietly, the PR officer accompanying Berry, conscious of the Green party's reputation for frugality and abstemiousness, cautioned her to stay away from anything resembling a hair shirt.

Berry continued to flick through, with barely suppressed excitement. But then she said: "I would not buy that white jacket!" Stepping forward with my notebook, I asked what ethical crime this particular garment represented. But it seemed I'd misunderstood. "Maintenance issues," she said with a shrug. "White's just not practical."

She chose an item she was happy with, made by Burberry, and stepped away to try it. Meanwhile the PR called Green HQ, only to be told that Burberry has used fur recently. And that wouldn't go down well with party members.

"I don't want to be the green police," she says. "My strategy is to look at the label. If something comes from a place where there might be a sweat-shop, I don't buy it. If it comes from within the EU it's probably good.

"People don't have the time, when they're buying a pair of socks, to find out how they were made. And I don't want people to have to do all that research. I want the Green Party to help people make that happen at a higher level – by passing laws. We can make it unprofitable for manufacturers to do the wrong thing. So the solution to consumers' ethical concerns is to vote for us."

So Berry chose something else, dressed, had her hair done and wandered with entourage towards Piccadilly Circus. A group of 10-year-old German girls, clocking the camera, asked for her autograph. "I did explain who I was," she said afterwards with becoming modesty. "But they didn't seem to mind."

Berry was Green candidate for Hampstead and Highgate in the general election of 2005. She lost. Likewise, she missed being elected to Camden Council in both the 2002 and 2006 local elections – and daily places a curse on first-past-the-post electoral system. But shortly before we met she was elected as the party's female "principal speaker".

Jenny Jones, a senior Green on the London Assembly, enthusiastically welcomed Berry's appointment. "Sian is brilliant. She is competent and energetic, and passionate. She comes across as fresh and people warm to her. She has a great grasp on the policy and she puts across a side to the party that you don't normally associate with us: she is attractive!"

Berry has piercing blue eyes, and blond hair hanging low over her shoulders. She somehow contrives to look willowy even when slouching and stretching blearily over her coffee. And her personal appearance has had quite an effect: The *Independent on Sunday* described her as "pure environmental viagra" and a "Green goddess".

But lest this give a false impression, Berry doesn't milk it. Arriving late to meet me, she looked ordinarily harassed and not the least bit pleased with herself – refreshingly unlike conventional politicians of either sex.

Berry was brought up in Cheltenham, where her parents were teachers. The oldest of three girls, she attended the local grammar. At Oxford, she studied materials science: many of her contemporaries went into the military industry, others into banking.

After Oxford, she came to London. From 1999 to 2003, she worked as trainee copywriter, simplifying medical and pharmaceutical issues for nurses and GPs. Most of the work involved lucrative lifestyle drugs: "Drugs for obesity, and the Viagra family of drugs. I was working to get people to want to use them. I was pretty cynical about it."

And she gradually became more political. "Look what happened during that period. The war in the Balkans, 9/11, the war in Afghanistan, and the build up to Iraq…" She started volunteering for the Green party, then joined up. "I got really excited trying to convert everybody."

As she soon found, most people haven't even heard of the Green party. Even those who have don't always know that it has policies unrelated to the environment.

In power, the Greens would get rid of Britain's nuclear, chemical and biological weapons. They would take the drug trade out of criminal control but regulate it, while banning advertising for alcohol and tobacco. They'd ban new out-of-town developments. Restore trade union rights and encourage cooperatives. Make the national curriculum voluntary. ("Education should be about developing human beings not economic units.") And they would pay a "citizen's income" to absolutely everybody, including children, to remove the dependency on benefits: with the income payable regardless of employment status, there'd be no point in doing nothing.

Berry spent a long time checking out the policies, she says, before joining the party. Then she resigned from her job and found a new one, at Imperial College, working on the medical faculty's website. She was taken on full time and that's where she works now, with a day off each week to devote to the Green party.

It was while travelling to work that she had the idea that made her name. "I was living in Highgate, and I used to stand every day at the bus stop during the school run. The streets were clogged with petrol-guzzling 4x4s. I thought, "Someone needs to do something about this." I went to find out who that someone was, but there was no one. I found that somebody in the US was doing something with leaflets on the cars. I thought I could do something similar. I was a copywriter, and I'd done some leaflets on giving up smoking, which is a similar problem, because people driving 4x4s know they are doing something wrong but don't have the will power to give up."

She drew up a spoof parking ticket, a truly inspired work of satire designed to resemble the real thing but packed with information about climate catastrophe. She took it to her local Greenpeace group. "They said, great, we will use this. We had a whip round and got 1,000 printed up. The local paper found some and did a story. It was the start of a media frenzy. I was one of the journalists who wrote about the "Alliance Against Urban 4x4s", as the group styled themselves. And I found the tickets so impressive that I sent off for some to put on the offending vehicles myself.

The media hoo-ha reached a peak as Berry took a holiday driving through Europe to Croatia. ("A lot of emissions, but not as much as flying.") She spent most of the time on the phone to journalists. "It cost me a fortune." When she got back, she went on Richard and Judy.

The actress Thandie Newton became a crusader against gas-guzzling cars after finding one of Berry's stickers on her 4x4. Newton traded in the offending vehicle for a hybrid Toyota Prius, and wrote letters to other celebrities urging them to do the same. They included: Madonna and Guy Ritchie, Jamie Oliver, Chris Martin, Barry Manilow, Wayne Rooney, and the Hollywood stars Kevin Costner, Bill Murray, Meg Ryan, Jack Nicholson, Ben Affleck and Tom Cruise.

"There can't be a Landcruiser or Cayenne driver in the country who hasn't had their ear bent by a public-spirited friend over dinner. These factors do seem to be making the 4×4 unfashionable at last."

It was the 4x4 campaign that won Berry her renown, and explains why the Green appointed her to her current position. But she'll need to work a miracle to make the party mainstream. In the European elections the Greens won more than a million votes, but they still don't have an MP at Westminster. If the next election is conducted under the current system, Berry concedes, they hope to win two seats in parliament, and move into second place in "at least" four others. Proportional representation is the party's best hope. "With PR, people would be much more free to vote for what they believe in, so I'd expect 10 per cent support, if not more, and at least 40 MPs."

Is a Green vote a wasted vote? "No. In places like Norwich and Brighton, our presence on the council is having a great effect. In Kirklees, they've managed to put up five per cent of the UK's solar panels on their houses."

In the meantime, while waiting to assume power, Greens like Berry must persuade the public – including people who will never vote Green – to change its habits. Take aviation. How will she stop people flying abroad for hen weekends? "We can't turn around to someone and say, I don't want you to go. When it comes to changing behaviour, you have to be positive. Talk about how good this country is. Dorset is incredibly trendy, and Cornwall. We need to get our own tourist industry going. We have some great beaches. And I have really fond memories of camping in the Lakes…" Not everybody, I fear, will be swayed by this.

While it's important to convey the terrible urgency about climate change, she says, "You have to show what people can do about it. Imagine the Green party as the person in the disaster movie who says, 'It's OK, I used to work in this building, I know the way out. Come with me…' We are really on top of climate change. This is something we've been thinking about for 30 years.

"There are some things we want to do that will cost money, but other things will save money. The government subsidises aviation to something like £9bn a year, and there's no real economic benefit. We would also cancel road building. At the moment we're spending £30bn on that. And Trident – that's another £25bn."

According to Berry, the catastrophe facing us requires a five per cent cut in emissions every year. The Conservatives say they will achieve a lot with green taxes. "But they're seeing it as a cash cow. You need to spend the money on ways to help make the green measures easier to comply with. Gordon Brown put £45 on road tax for 4x4s but that's not enough, it's not going to change anybody's behaviour."

Just after this, we left the health-food shop and Berry started rolling up her cigarette. At the time, I hadn't thought this a big deal – it's none of my business if she smokes. But after talking to her friend Blake Ludwig, a Greenpeace man who helped with the anti-4x4 campaign, I began to wonder if it might be a problem after all.

"I'm always on her case about smoking," Ludwig told me. "She says she plans to give up and she knows it's bad."

I asked if he knew that she'd previously written guides to help people give up. He didn't.

Of course he didn't. She didn't mention those guides, because they plainly didn't have any effect on her own smoking habit. So how can Berry hope to change other people's behaviour if she can't change her own?

chapter 16

A well known petrol-head has a custard pie shoved in his face

---

I liked Berry, and wished her every success. But her suggestion that "the solution" was to vote Green had the same miserable implications as all other party-political boasting: it endorsed the disempowering conceit that "there's only so much we can do as individuals", that only government can save us – and that one bunch of people are right and the others are all wrong.

The Green party had not been particularly successful just yet, but I worried that if it did get people elected they would fall into the unhelpful habits of all professional politicians, who cheerfully dismiss a good idea only because a rival party came up with it.

Faced with climate change and peak oil, it seemed to me that it was time to stop dividing the world into "them and us"?

The question was thrown into relief when I was asked to interview a well known petrolhead, Jeremy Clarkson, after he had a custard pie shoved in his face by an anti-road protestor.

Clarkson had anticipated some kind of attack, he told me. Addressing an assembly of engineering students at Oxford Brookes University, he began: "I fully expected to be speaking to you today covered in flour and eggs, like a giant human pancake."

The Top Gear presenter had come to collect an honorary degree, awarded in recognition of his long-standing support for engineering. Only after his speech finished was his dire prediction fulfilled – give or take the odd ingredient – by a woman named Becky Lush.

Clarkson had disappeared into a marquee, Lush remembers. "But then he came out again, so I ran after him." Catching up, she leapt high in the air and copped the Motoring Writer of the

Year in the face with a home-made, organic banana meringue. In case you imagined otherwise, that's not as easy as it sounds: "He's a bloody huge guy, six-foot-four: hitting him in the face was like playing basketball."

Having completed her mission, Lush, 33, kept moving. "I had to run very fast from a security guard. I don't know what you can be charged with, legally, for putting a pie on someone – and I had no idea what Clarkson might do."

In the event, Clarkson's response was generous. He congratulated his assailant: "Great shot!" The only criticism he offered, while the assembled photographers happily snapped away, was to state that the meringue tasted too sweet.

"It's unfortunate that I was terribly jet-lagged," he says now. "Otherwise, I would have guessed that something was up when the photographers said, 'Would you mind stepping over there, because the light is better…?' They knew what was going on. And I have to say that, at the PR level, it was a fantastic result for the environmentalists. One-nil to them."

But how did it come to this? How did Clarkson, who brings joy to so many, become the bete noir of the environmental movement? Why did thousands sign a petition urging Oxford Brookes to withdraw the honour? And what motivated this particular woman to do more than sign up – to bake a banana meringue and convey it far from home to sully the face and robes of a man she'd never met?

Clarkson was nominated for the degree by the School of Technology, for supporting high standards in engineering – something he did most notably by championing Brunel as the "Greatest Briton" in 2002; and, as a passenger on the last BA Concorde flight a year later, by paraphrasing Neil Armstrong to describe the retirement of that engineering classic: "This is one small step for a man, but one huge leap backwards for mankind".

But his work has also earned him the hatred of the green movement. On Top Gear Clarkson drove through virgin peat bogs in a 4×4 and tore up road safety information on camera. Racing against colleagues, he drove a Ferrari more or less non-stop from London to Switzerland, regardless of fatigue, and was stopped by police for speeding. And the BBC was obliged to pay £250 in compensation to a parish council in Somerset after Clarkson deliberately rammed a Toyota pick-up into a 30-year-old horse chestnut.

Clarkson – technically my colleague because we both work for *The Sunday Times* – was unrepentant. "The parish council is funded by central government, which is funded by me, so it's my tree. Anyway, there was no damage."

Environmentalists believe that what Clarkson says and does on screen encourages others to copy him. He recently vowed to kill cyclists "for fun" if they failed to respect the Highway Code – a promise that has provoked furious debate on the pages of cycling magazines and websites, where Clarkson is always pictured quaffing champagne on that last Concorde flight. But he refuses to accept that he's a role model. "When people say that to me, I ask, 'Would you do something, just because I did it?' And they always say no. And I say, 'Well, if you wouldn't, then why do you think someone else would?'"

It was a good point. I had left spoof parking tickets on 4x4s, directly inspired by Sian Berry, but I had not chosen to copy her habit of smoking cigarettes.

In Lush, Clarkson was confronted by someone whose obsession with cars, though less well known than his, has been no less consuming. The main difference between them is that Clarkson loves motor vehicles, and Lush hates them.

In 1993, Lush was jailed for four months for her part in protests against road building on Twyford Down. "It wasn't nice. But the support we got was incredible. It was the first time environmental activists had been sent to prison, and it really inspired people. I received 100 letters a day."

Her motivation has always been climate change. "I love the countryside and I love nature, but I don't see global warming as a countryside thing. It's about the survival of our species. It's about people. And transport is the fastest-growing contributor to climate change."

Like many activists, Lush eased off after Labour came to power in 1997. "We stepped back because we had won. Labour came to power and said, 'No more roads.' And John Prescott set up his commission for integrated transport." So she moved into campaigning against genetically modified crops, and got a job driving a bus.

But around the time of the fuel protests of 2000, the government seemed to change its mind on transport issues, and Lush became active again. She set up an anti-roads alliance, Road Block, and began chucking pies. She put one in the face of the US envoy to environmental talks at the Hague, and another on the transport secretary, subsequently Chancellor of the Exchequer, Alistair Darling.

More recently, she chained herself to a digger for over two hours before a specialist team removed her. And she reduced to chaos a meeting to discuss the planned Thames Gateway Bridge public inquiry by snatching the inspector's microphone and shouting, as she was chased around a table: "This is a scandal. The bridge is being railroaded through. You are not listening to people."

And I have to say that I personally consider these achievements entirely admirable. But some might argue that it's childish. Not at all, Lush insists. "You grab attention through direct action. I don't think people would have thought about these issues otherwise. Direct action is about making people think, 'Why is that woman doing that?' People thought we were weird, in 1992, to risk our lives by standing in front of bulldozers. But environmentalists are always putting out messages that we're derided for until, ten to fifteen years later, the ideas have become mainstream."

With some pride, she adds that the Master of the Rolls, Lord Hoffman, told her in the early 90s that "civil disobedience in this country is an honourable tradition, and that those who take part in it may be vindicated by history". (All the same, he rejected her appeal against imprisonment.)

And what about Clarkson? Will he ever be reconciled with the Greens? "I don't want to be their bete noir," he insists. "I want to be the champion of ordinary people – who seem to be lectured to all the time. Look, there are two sides to the argument. I do listen, constantly, to their side of the argument. And every time they're presented with my side, they shove pies in my face." Not literally, of course, but here's what he means: "I went on Jeremy Vine's radio show to discuss some aspect of the environment and they had the environmentalist George Monbiot on, and he said, on air, that if I liked 4×4s it must be because my penis is small! He sent me a letter afterwards apologising for getting carried away, but if that's the level of debate…

"You do have to be bonkers to drive a 4×4 in cities, absolutely. You have to be clinically insane, properly Loony Tunes mad. But it's no business of anyone else.

"They get together to discuss things, these people, eating their nuclear-free peace nibbles, and they're just never exposed to the other side of the argument. They say, 'We live in Hackney and we think such-and-such a thing is wrong.' And that's it.

"There is no doubt that we will all have to subscribe to their views, eventually. In fact, to judge by the pie incident, the time has already passed."

chapter 17

Richard Gere, the Hollywood actor, observes that we are "all in the same boat", and inspires the author to look into Buddhism

My conversations with Berry, Clarkson and Lush had left me confused. Does one person set an example to others, or not? Must everything be adversarial? If one side "wins", how does the other lot feel?

A meeting with Richard Gere, the Hollywood actor, gave me some clues.

My first sight of Gere, who won People magazine's Sexiest Man Alive award as recently as 1999, was in the studios of Holland's third public TV channel, where he shuffled into the light and blinked at the audience that surrounded him. He wore jeans and a black, ribbed sweater that gave an impression of paunchiness. His hair was not the familiar silver, but white, and the harsh studio lights, shining through it with forensic attention, acquainted the cameras with a surprisingly pink scalp. On top of that he wore long-sight glasses that everybody knows look bad on telly: they cast heavy shadows and shimmering puddles of light over his cheeks.

This couldn't be an accident. He was making a deliberate statement: forget the movie star, meet the other Richard Gere.

He'd come to the Netherlands to accept an award on behalf of the International Campaign for Tibet, of which he's chairman. The Geuzen Medal honours the ICT for promoting human rights and self-determination in Tibet through non-violent means. While he was here, Gere was throwing himself into political affairs: urging the European Union to stop France and Germany lifting the arms embargo on China that was imposed after the events in

Tiananmen Square in 1989. Why? Because China occupies Tibet, and its human rights record remains poor.

That's what he spoke about this afternoon, at a press conference attended by the main Dutch media. He also took questions, mostly inane. Tonight he hoped to speak in greater depth. B&W is a highbrow chat show, with a formidable woman presenter, Hanneke Groenteman. Gere talked about many things, including Buddhism and Tibet ("the ancient wisdom culture… is the country's greatest export") and about Tibetans who lose fingers and toes, perhaps even children, as they escape across the cold mountains to Nepal.

When Groenteman pressed him about China he avoided criticism, insisted he does not wish unpleasantness on the Chinese or anybody else, and touched on the Buddhist concept of karma. "We're all in the same boat here, all of us – Hitler, the Chinese, you, me… If anything, the Chinese are creating horrendous future lifetimes for themselves, and one cannot fail to be compassionate towards them for that."

All human beings are connected with one another, he added, and to underline the point he stared warmly into Groenteman's eyes and placed a hand on hers.

This was not the idiom of current affairs. Groenteman deflated the poetic mood by placing her other hand on top of Gere's: "Thank you, your Holiness," she said.

To be a celebrity, these days, you must do charity work and be seen doing it. But Gere has done that for years, and gone beyond the call of duty. In 1993, as presenter of an Academy Award, he declared: "If something miraculous, really kind of movie-like could happen here… [Deng Xiaoping] will take the Chinese away from Tibet." He asked a billion viewers to beam "love and truth and a kind of sanity" to China's then-premier. Not exactly firebrand rhetoric, but enough to put Gere among the small minority of performers who have turned political at the Oscars. He was banned from appearing there again.

Henry Kissinger, who secured détente between the US and China in the 1970s, said at the time, "Richard Gere is a better actor than he is a political analyst'". Some fans disapprove too. On an Internet site I found this recent diatribe, aimed specifically at

Gere: "These actors make me sick. I think it's time for them to keep their political agenda to themselves. If you don't like it here, go to Tibet or other countries that flip your trigger. We don't need you here." Even the Dalai Lama's Special Envoy, Lodi Gyari, was unsure about Gere initially. (Gyari is executive chairman of the ICT.) "But as soon as I got to know Richard as a person, as a friend," Gyari told me, "my cynicism disappeared. He has a deep spiritual commitment." The composer Philip Glass, who co-founded New York's Tibet House with Gere, to help preserve Tibetan culture, says he brought energy and intelligence to the project. He also inspired others to join the cause, including Harrison Ford, Sharon Stone and Goldie Hawn.

Gere doesn't restrict his activism to Tibet. He went to the West Bank, as part of his general commitment to pacifism, backing plans to show an Arabic version of Richard Attenborough's film, Gandhi. He persuaded contacts to put together safe-sex TV ads in India: the prime minister hosted meetings, Bill Gates contributed $2.4m, and James Murdoch, head of satellite network Star India, donated $14m in airtime. But Julia Taft, who worked closely with Gere on Tibet as assistant secretary of state in the Clinton administration, believes that cause is different from the rest. "His interest in Tibetan culture and Buddhism is particularly important and effective. He did go to Kosovo," she recalled, "but it didn't raise awareness because – well, my sense is that he understood it less and had less passion, even though he did it in good faith."

I have to confess that when I was assigned to interview Gere I was not overwhelmed with joy. At some unspoken level I suspected he was shallow and self-regarding. There was little justification for this: I knew little about him except that he was regarded as a "difficult" interview, and out of some barmy, misplaced solidarity with other journalists, I took Gere's "difficulty" as an affront to my people. I decided I would not be impressed by him.

But I was. How to explain all the work he does, despite the flak he gets from journalists, politicians and others? It could only be this: he believes in it. And he didn't show any of the inclination, shared by Berry, Lush, Clarkson and professional politicians – to rubbish the opposition.

The morning after his interview on B&W, Gere hosted a working breakfast at his hotel with Gyari and a Dutch MP, Boris Dittrich. Dittrich, who speaks perfect English, has a history of supporting Tibet, and the ICT wants to encourage that. Gyari describes the latest talks with Beijing as the most serious so far. As the Dalai Lama has stated, the issue is not Tibetan independence from China but genuine autonomy; the model could be Hong Kong.

Clearly, Dittrich could receive such a briefing without Gere coming along, but would politicians like him bother to meet the Tibetans without him there? Perhaps they would, but the presence of a Hollywood star makes such encounters more appealing.

In fact, Gere doesn't merely bring people together. He also speaks incisively. The Geuzen award is usually presented by Dutch royalty. This year the job has fallen to a local politician, perhaps because of pressure from China. Gere asks: "Is it worth making some point that the royal family didn't get involved this year...?"

"Yes," Dittrich replies, "but maybe only if journalists raise the question first."

As they rise from the table, Dittrich says: "This has been very useful. Thank you." "Thank you," says Gere. "There are very few people willing to be seen with us." That's not quite true – since the Dalai Lama won the Nobel Peace Prize, in 1989, the Tibetan cause has been rather fashionable – but it flatters Dittrich, so what's the harm?

"I would like to show the Chinese that I'm completely independent," the MP adds, a little slavishly.

"You know what would be good for me?" Gere asks. "If you were to say to the Chinese, 'Mr Gere spoke to me about Tibet but he was very respectful about China. I expected to get this rant about China but not at all...'"

"Yes, that is the most effective way."

"It's also true. I had this conversation with my Palestinian friends, who are flirting with non-violence. I told them, it's not a tactic. It's real. If it's not, then it won't work."

I found this sentence rather stunning, because it's so obviously true but also generally overlooked.

Leaving the room, the MP's assistant gushes: "You have really raised awareness." Gere smiles. "That's my job." But it's not his day job. And though his starry presence may bring politicians – and journalists – wherever Gere goes, I can't help wondering if Hollywood will always eclipse Tibet. One upmarket Dutch broadsheet, I notice, carries a report on yesterday's press conference... on its "Entertainment" pages.

Would Gere be taken more seriously if he gave up acting? Went into politics, like Arnold Schwarzenegger? He laughs, actually throwing his head back. It's the most animated I've seen him, but lasts a mere fraction of a second. "I like Arnold. He is a really interesting guy, and potentially he can have an enormous impact. But I don't think he thought of himself as an actor." Ouch.

That afternoon, we travel out of Amsterdam towards the town of Vlaardingen, for the award ceremony. A huge crowd has assembled around the town church, mostly composed of young-to middle-aged women waving camera phones. There's a military band, sea cadets holding wreaths for VIPs to lay at a war memorial. From the top of the church flies a Tibetan flag. Gere looks his best again. He steps forward with Gyari to place a wreath, then they clasp hands in what I take to be Buddhist fashion.

Inside, the church is sober. There's a great wooden pulpit, from which hangs a portrait of the Dalai Lama. Every available space is covered with seats, reserved for eminent citizens. Gyari is invited onstage to accept a medal and a scroll on behalf of the ICT. He makes a speech. There's a poem from a Dutch schoolgirl, then a Tibetan woman steps up to hoist a three-stringed instrument across her front. "I am going to sing an auspicious song for this happy occasion..." she announces.

Finally Gere is called up to make his own speech. "This is an incredibly moving experience," he begins. "From a Tibetan point of view, just to be born human is extremely difficult and rare. It's a great responsibility. And there is nothing that gives a human life more meaning than caring for each other." He describes the situation in Tibet, the perils of the trip across the mountains, the need for political action.

"Just for a second, I would like everyone in this room to close their eyes and say, 'I personally will do what I can.'" At that moment, church bell ring the hour. "I liked that," he grins. "It was nice. I will take that as 'Amen'. So I'm going to consider us all brothers and sisters. We have a secret society in our hearts. And this brotherhood and sisterhood is going to change society. Thank you."

There's huge applause. Gere leads Gyari towards the exit. As soon as he's outside, a substantial choir of female voices shakes off the burden of Dutch sobriety to let out an appreciative whoop.

Gere was born 1949 and grew up in New York state, the second of five children. His father, Homer, sold insurance and his mother, Doris, stayed at home. Richard was musical, but his first ambition was to be an Olympic gymnast. He won a gymnastics scholarship to the University of Massachusetts in Amherst, but left after two years to pursue acting.

He played Danny Zuko in Grease in New York, in 1973, then in London. (Many people forgot, when he sang and danced in the film of Chicago – for which he won a Golden Globe and an Oscar nomination – that he'd done something like it before.) His screen career also took off, almost in spite of his judgement. "The two movies that I didn't want to do, but I had mortgage payments coming up and whatever, were An Officer and a Gentleman and Pretty Woman." (The latter was the highest-grossing film of 1990.) One lucrative part he did turn down was the lead in Die Hard, which went instead to Bruce Willis.

Off screen, Gere married the supermodel Cindi Crawford in 1991 and divorced her in 1995. Then he met the actress Carey Lowell, another Buddhist, often described as a "Bond girl" since she appeared in Licence to Kill. Gere and Lowell have a young son, Homer. Gere finds it hard, he tells me, to wrench himself away from them "I would never have taken the red-eye from the US before, because you're so tired afterwards. Now, I don't want to miss him – so I fly while he's asleep."

So much for the public and the personal life. What about his spiritual career? Gere grew up in a "serious, churchgoing" Methodist family. At university, he studied philosophy ("I remember being stunned by Bishop Berkeley's idea that reality is a function of the mind," he tells me. "There is nothing 'out there'."). In his 20s he discovered Buddhism.

Nicholas Vreeland, a Buddhist monk, has been Gere's friend since 1980. In 1993, Vreeland accompanied Gere on a trip that would profoundly influence the actor. "He had been outspoken," Vreeland recalls, "and the Chinese government decided to show Richard that they were good guys. They invited him to show a movie he had produced." Gere asked Vreeland and their teacher, the Reverend Khyongla Rato Rinpoche, to come with him and won permission to visit Tibet. It was the first time Gere had been, and the first time Rinpoche had returned to his monastery since fleeing Tibet, in 1959, with the Dalai Lama. "The townspeople poured out to greet him," Vreeland recalls. "They lined up with white scarves, lit incense and... well, Tibetans stick their tongues out in politeness and they did that too. The whole town was there. These people were hungry for some kind of spiritual touch and enlightenment. Richard was overwhelmed, as we all were."

Can Vreeland describe Gere's own progress in Buddhism? "Well, he devotes more and more of his time to things that help others, and less to pursuing his own selfish desires. He is a happy person. He has a level of contentment. There is also a wisdom about him, a philosophical attitude – you can only do so much, you must do your best. I think that is a reflection of his [Buddhist] practice."

We're at Gere's hotel when I sit down to speak with him, one to one. I say I'd like to talk about Tibet, Buddhism and acting. Almost immediately he launches into a speech that I find incomprehensible. "You have to ask, what is real and what is the mind?" he begins. "Is there really a separation between you and me?" As if to make this clearer, he moves a pair of glasses around: one represents me, I guess, the other Gere. "Is it true that you and me are here?"

I must be looking baffled because he stops, sighs, throws up his arms. "You will never print this! I've been doing interviews for so long... for 25 years. You'll never use this."

My heart sinks. Gere hates interviews. Journalists have found him hard work: "The most miserable, insular and self-obsessed actor it has been my misfortune to meet", one wrote. All too often, interviews are terminated after somebody goes too far. Some have asked if it's true that Gere once waved his penis at a woman reporter (he doesn't remember). Others inquire about his short-lived marriage to Crawford, and the ill-judged newspaper ad they placed in *The New York Times*, insisting that everything was fine and, bizarrely, that both were heterosexual. (He's said lawyers advised them to do it, and he wouldn't do it again.)

The fact is that Gere has attracted a huge amount of sexual innuendo over the years. And it's easy to understand his frustration when that becomes the focus of an interview. But he seemed to expect it even before our chat started.

To his credit – and my relief – he starts again. "The biggest habit of mind is self. We think about ourselves: me, then my family, then my village, then my country..."

I think I understand, now. He's pleading for people to love one another, as he did with Groenteman on TV last night. Hoping to ingratiate myself, I tell him, correctly but irrelevantly, that my mother's family background is Quaker, so I'm sympathetic to his interest in non-violence. From now on his attitude changes. He visibly relaxes, and we continue to talk for some 90 minutes.

I ask about meditation. "I started to practise Zen when I was 24. The core is to sit and follow the breathing. Concentrate on the breathing. Not in a hard way, but count to ten, count the exhalations to ten. If you lose count then catch yourself and say, 'Oh, I'm thinking again.' And bring yourself back to the breathing. Eventually you get to the point where you are just breathing. Almost all forms of meditation are a form of looking at the mind. In the beginning you are almost amazed how much noise is going on there. You have no idea how much monkey stuff is going on, how cluttered it is. You look at that and you're acknowledging what the mind is, you're taming it, and when you have done that you have learned the power of concentration."

Unlike most Buddhists, Gere sees the Dalai Lama privately several times a year. The meetings are not always easy. "I've had to explain to people who have a romantic vision of His Holiness that at times he's been cross with me. I'm not saying it was pleasant, but I'm thankful that he trusts me enough to not pull any punches. Mind you, the first meetings were not that way; he was aware how fragile I was and he was very careful."

At their first meeting, the Dalai Lama asked him about acting. "He said, 'When you do this acting and you're angry, are you really angry? When you're acting sad, are you really sad?' I gave him an actor's answer. I said, it's more effective if you really believe in the emotion you portray. He looked deeply into my eyes laughed. Hysterically. He was laughing at the idea that I could believe emotions are real – that I would work so hard to believe in anger and hatred and sadness and pain and suffering.

"I should have known, as an actor, that I create those emotions. And that is what we all do, every day."

chapter 18

The author submits himself as pupil to a Vietnamese Zen monk

I came away from meeting Gere liberated from my old feeling that eastern religion was silly, at any rate not appropriate for westerners. I had not even realised till I met him that to be a Buddhist does not require belief in God. I'd read as much in a useful short guide, *Buddhism Without Beliefs*, before meeting him. I loved that book, read it twice, then went directly against a lifetime's habit by giving it away because I wanted somebody else to benefit.

I wanted to find out more about Buddhism but didn't know where to begin. I had friends who were Buddhists, I'd been to their Buddhist wedding and found the chanting a teeny bit odd – but I'd not been in touch for a while and would have felt a bit odd calling up and saying, tell me about Buddhism. They belonged to an international movement that started in Japan, and I noticed that the man who sold me a piano, found for me some time before by Asha, advertised the group's events in his shop window. But I didn't ask him either.

So I read a little online, and flicked through books in shops, but soon became overwhelmed once more by the feeling that it wasn't for me. I couldn't get my head round the differences between the many different traditions – Zen, Pure Land, Theravada, and many more; or indeed the seemingly endless ideas that were categorised, presumably for somebody's convenience, by number. So far as I could tell, adherents recognised Two Truths, Three Dharma Seals, Three Doors of Liberation, Four Noble Truths, Five Aggregates, Six Paramitas, Seven Factors of Awakening, a Noble Eightfold Path, and Twelve Links of Independent Co-Arising, whatever that was. I couldn't begin to imagine getting my head around all that.

But then one day I popped into the offices of a publishing company and saw a vast heap of books by a man I'd never heard of before: Thich Nhat Hanh.

I picked up a book and read a quote on the jacket: "Thich Nhat Hanh is a holy man, for he is humble and devout. He is a scholar of immense intellectual capacity." The words were written by Martin Luther King, in nominating Thich Nhat Hanh for the Nobel Peace Prize.

King died in 1968, which meant that Thich Nhat Hanh had been nominated for the Nobel forty or more years ago, and I'd still never heard of him. My intellectual interest – or pride – was piqued. I read on. "Thich Nhat Hanh is one of the most beloved Buddhist teachers in the West," wrote a certain Joanna Macy, "a rare combination of mystic, poet, scholar and activist. His luminous presence and the simple compassionate clarity of his writings have touched countless lives."

It could hardly hurt to try his book. It only had 140 pages, and the print was fairly large too.

So I did. And the effect was as great as those quotes seemed to promise. I was blown away by the simplicity of what was written, which urged readers gently and warmly to enjoy the here and now.

The secret was to approach all of life like meditation – including the bits we think of as boring or unpleasant. "Every act is a rite," he says at one point.

> While washing the dishes one should only be washing the dishes, which means that while washing the dishes one should be completely aware of the fact that one is washing the dishes. At first glance, that might seem a little silly: why put so much stress on a simple thing? But that's precisely the point. The fact that I'm washing these bowls is a wondrous reality... If while washing dishes we think only of the cup of tea that awaits us, thus hurrying to get the dishes out of the way as if they were a nuisance, we are not "washing the dishes to wash the dishes". What's more we are not alive

during the time we are washing the dishes. In fact we are completely incapable of realising the miracle of life while standing at the sink. If we can't wash the dishes, the chances are we won't be able to drink our tea either. While drinking the cup of tea, we will only be thinking of other things, barely aware of the cup in our hands. Thus we are sucked away into the future – and we are incapable of actually living one minute of life.

This was more like it: washing dishes, and drinking tea, proved a lot easier to get my head round. And I could see how it could be applied more widely – how by fretting about climate change or peak oil or rubbish piling up in landfill or people working in sweatshops I might fail to be "alive" to the good things available here and now in the present.

It also made me think, over the following weeks and months, that every one of the tasks that we have learned to outsource could potentially be as rewarding as washing up. And that would have to include making clothes.

Of course, it wasn't all about washing up. Quite a substantial portion of the book was about breathing and being completely aware of breathing, which is certainly less remarkable as a message of personal transformation than the story of the Immaculate Conception, or the Crucifixion.

But that was exactly what I liked about Thich Nhat Hanh: he didn't put forward difficult ideas, or exotica, or anything unverifiable. What's could be easier to verify, and to put your faith in, than your own breathing?

People usually consider walking on water or in thin air a miracle. But I think the real miracle is not to walk either on water or in thin air, but to walk on earth. Every day we are engaged in a miracle which we don't even recognise: a blue sky, white clouds, green leaves, the black, curious eyes of a child – our own two eyes. All is a miracle.

I read that book in one sitting, then read it again, then went out and bought several more by the same author. I started reading bits out loud to Harriet, who listened politely and even seemed to take it in.

But what I wanted to know this: if I spend the whole time being "alive' – concentrating on the washing up and breathing and whatever else might be going on from one minute to the next – isn't that the same as burying my head in the sand about the real problems facing us, such as climate change? Isn't it right, sometimes, to stare into the middle distance and bite your nails, oblivious to the blue sky and white clouds, as you plot to change government policy, or design a high-spec solar panel?

chapter 19

Part of the problem or part of the solution?

At the same time, I was still struggling with something the man from Friends of the Earth had said: that there's "only so much we can do as individuals", and that some things can only be handled by government.

I was coming to the conclusion that this was incorrect – a conclusion reinforced when somebody told me a joke he'd heard on the radio, or maybe the telly – it doesn't matter which.

It went like this: "My dad shat himself last week – and the council still haven't been around to clean him up."

It's not a pleasant joke, perhaps not even a joke at all. But as an observation, an insight into how hopelessly dependent we have become on external authority – and grumpily, resentfully dependent, at that – it's hard to beat.

People have always organised themselves into systems of government to address large-scale issues, and that should continue. But government today is too big, and saps our potential as human beings.

People on state support find themselves trapped by the benefit system, unable even to try to work lest they lose their income, and thus deprived of the opportunity to do something that could give them self-worth.

Doctors, police officers, teachers and others are unable to exercise discretion and professional judgement, and must instead pursue government targets and directives that often directly undermine the services they provide. Schools, for instance, are under pressure to keep truancy rates low. As a result, rather than gradually work to improve a child's attendance, they're more likely to expel him. Police officers across the country are expected to bring down knife crime by a certain percentage – a baffling target for police in villages where knife-crime is non-existent, but one they must still put work into "addressing".

The micro-management is expensive, and seemingly without limit. In London, buses are fitted with pre-recorded messages announcing to passengers which stop they've arrived at – depriving drivers of one small personal service they could provide for any passengers who ask for help – and reducing them more than ever to the status of mere robots.

Every day, especially on "political" news and in the papers, we hear somebody angrily call on the government to "do something" and criticising the government for failing in its duties – in the process concealing the fact that we could do something ourselves.

If anybody makes a fuss about this, the government cracks down. For instance, as part of its drive to tackle crime, and terrorism in particular, the government made it illegal to protest outside parliament without prior permission, which undermines its own argument that the mark of a free country is one where anybody can go into the town square and exercise free speech. To highlight this inconsistency, groups of protestors held tea parties on Parliament Square and were arrested. One woman was arrested merely for reading out the names of people killed in Iraq.

When did we lose the capacity to protest, to determine our own workload, to clean up incontinent elders? When did we get the idea that government and its representatives should take care of these things – and nearly everything else? When did we start to believe that there is "only so much we can do as individuals", and meekly bestow our futures into other people's hands? Why did we let it happen? And more to the point, do we need to remain so hopelessly incapable, or can we take back control?

Tom Hodgkinson thinks we can throw off our shackles, and we must. In his brilliant book *How To Be Free*, he writes:

> Politics is not the art of running a country, it is the art of persuading the people that they need a set of paid politicians to run the country. And in this dark art, our leaders are skilled and proficient.

In order to keep themselves in power, they need to sell us the idea of themselves as our saviours and also to sell us the idea that we could not run things without them. In other words, they simply need to convince us that we are stupid and helpless. And this is what they work so hard to do. This is achieved principally by constant media coverage. Every newspaper, every radio bulletin, every TV news show, every news-based website: they are all crammed to bursting with coverage of party politics. It is the kind of free publicity that a PR for a private company can only dream of.

What can we do? Well, we can start simply by ignoring government. The best way to smash the state is to take no notice of it and hope it goes away. We are constantly told by the media that not voting is a sign of 'apathy', while to me it is a sign of the absolute opposite. When you do not vote, as I don't, then something fundamental shifts in your psyche. You can no longer blame the government for your problems, as you have opted out of their system.

You start to act for yourself. You become responsible.

Rousing stuff, though I'm not sure that he's right about the venality of politicians: most of them mean well, I believe, and if you listen carefully you can hear them suggest that we should take back control of our lives. But that message is lost as they score points against each other – and anyway they are unlikely to give up central control as long as they believe we will blame them when things go wrong.

Others might believe he's wrong more generally. They'd say that some problems are too big and complicated for individuals to fix – the economy, national security, crime? But I'm with Hodgkinson. Even those seemingly overwhelming problems can be addressed at the individual, or neighbourhood level.

As I write, for instance, the world economy is falling to pieces because money has basically disappeared. This is bad news only to people who don't realise that they can issue their own money.

Historically, in small towns, this was done by a few trusted individuals writing post-dated cheques – basically IOUs, just like "real" banknotes – which created economic activity until they were finally cashed, whereupon somebody wrote out new ones.

In the depression of the 1930s, people all over the world did this kind of thing: the notes were "backed" by the reputation of the issuers (again, just like banknotes). A group of businesses in Switzerland set up a "currency", called Wir, which is still going today; its members now include nearly a quarter of all Swiss businesses.

In the UK, this kind of thing is usually known as a barter network, and overcomes the big problem with what most people think of as barter: a direct, two-way swap. In that kind of barter, if I want one of your home-made cakes, but you don't want me to cut your hair, the trade wouldn't happen. But if I pay you a credit for your cake, you can spend it one somebody else in the network whose haircutting skills you respect. Which is to say: you don't need government money to get along, you only need a network of trustworthy neighbours with a variety of skills, who can mutually back a currency all of your own.

As for terrorism: if you have neighbours who look dodgy, you could either phone the police and report them, or invite them round for tea and let them have their say, thereby showing that the ordinary members of the public are decent and generous, and do not deserve to be bombed. This small gesture could be enough to keep a would-be terrorist from actually doing any harm.

A similar approach can be taken to street crime. If you see a group of dodgy youths, give them a smile. One young woman who used to mug people on buses once told me that she always got violent when she saw that people expected that of her. And she stopped mugging people when one woman she was trying to rob bravely asked her to get off the bus and accompany her to a place where she could get help.

Then again, you can offer yourself as a mentor to young people who lack decent role models: the American mentoring programme,

Big Brothers, Big Sisters, has phenomenal effects on participants: young people with mentors are significantly less likely to go off the rails than others.

Or by training as a mediator, you can intervene in disputes between neighbours before they escalate. The barrister Stephen Ruttle QC took me to lunch once and explained how this works. "I have had 25 years of hammering people in the witness box," he said. "I'm a Christian and I thought, this can't be the right way to resolve things."

Ruttle's wife suggested he should go on a mediation course. ("Something that litigators regard as a bit like quiche," he says, "soft and squidgy and unappealing.") But he did as she suggested. "I was blown away. In 80 to 85 per cent of cases that go to mediation settle by agreement. That's an amazing difference." Professionally, he's now a full-time mediator. He uses the skills outside work too, in the south-London borough where he lives.

"The criminal justice system imposes a solution from outside. Mediation turns that on its head. You go into someone's flat on the 16th floor of a tower block and they're full of pain. These people were posting crap through each other's doors. You go from one flat to the next, and if they agree, you get them to meet on a neutral venue and you say that you don't have the solution. And they work it out between them.

"It doesn't always work. That particular case was incredibly tense for 15 minutes, but then one of the men leaned over the table and – I will never forget this – he said, 'Would it help if...' And the response was, 'Yeah, if you do that, I'll do this...' When you sit people down together extraordinary things can happen."

Another mediator, Maria Arpa, told me that a murder costs the Home Office £1.1m, on average, excluding healthcare costs, whereas a high-level mediation dealing with gangs over several months would cost £10,000 to £20,000.

How would that work? "In a case like this, you would probably not bring the two sides face to face but shuttle between them. One side might say that the other has tricked them, or been selling drugs on their patch, so they're going to kill someone. So you say, 'And what happens when they come back and kill you, or your little brother?' And they haven't thought about that. Then you go and see the other side and ask them to stay out of the area while you're negotiating, and you gradually get them to agree certain things in principle.

"You might not get them away from crime altogether, in these cases, but you stop that particular killing and you gradually get the whole family involved, because the mothers don't want their children to be killed.

"What happens over time is that they trust you, and they understand that you're not the police, and they actually call you in to mediate. Someone might phone you and say, 'So-and-so is going to be killed at a certain club on Saturday.' So you start mediating at once."

Even if you're a victim of violence yourself, you can make a difference. Through a restorative justice scheme, the financier Will Riley was able to meet a career criminal, Peter Woolf, who had broken into his home and injured him, and confront him with what he did.

The meeting took place in prison, Riley told me. "The criminal walked in, looking sheepish. However, he soon started talking social-work bollocks, parrot fashion. I was thinking: "This is getting nowhere." Then he looked at me and said: 'When we met…' And I lost it.

"I said: 'We didn't meet at some cocktail party. You broke into my house and hit me on the head.' And it all came out, everything I was feeling – about how terrible it was not to be able to protect my family. Stuff I hadn't even told my wife. I hadn't really known how I felt until it just came out, like water from a fire hydrant. Afterwards, I was exhausted – but when I got home I knew there wouldn't be anyone behind my front door."

Hearing this hit the criminal, Peter Woolf, like a bombshell. "We could see that," Riley said. "He was gutted. And you don't leave somebody who's in that kind of state, not unless you're a shit, so we spent about 10 minutes talking about how to help him. We said we wanted him to write to us every six months and tell us what he was doing. And I told him that if he went back to his old life, he'd be shitting on our goodwill."

People think restorative justice sounds easy, Riley said, but it's not. "It's very hard to confront somebody. But I believe you should meet and talk to criminals because that re-empowers you." Today, Peter Woolf is a reformed man, and Riley considers him a friend: I know this, because I met them both, together, and that kind of warm friendship is hard to fake.

So if you have dodgy-looking neighbours, or hoodies on your street corner, go and say hello. Get them round for tea. Sign them up to your barter network.

Because if you're not providing the solution, you may be part of the problem.

PART
TWO

chapter 20

The author uploads a video to Threadbangers

In an idle moment, I got out my camcorder and set it up in the office in my loft. I put on an expensive shirt I'd bought when I worked in a proper office and wore a tie. It was from Thomas Pink, one of many like it, and didn't fit me as well as it should. I knew that because long ago I'd treated myself to that fitted shirt at Brooks Brothers.

So I got out the camcorder, set the light and the sound and the focus, and pressed record.

"Hi, my name's John-Paul. I need some help with my shirts. They've got big necks – you can see why – and that makes them really baggy and I want to take them in."

I stopped recording, put on the fitted shirt, and started again.

"I had this shirt made for me. It's the only one I've ever had made for me. It fits beautifully, feels incredibly comfortable. But it cost a fortune. How can I get another one made without paying the same money. Can I make it myself? Do I take it apart, or just copy it onto a piece of paper?"

I plugged the camera into my computer, and emailed the clip to ThreadBangers, a weekly programme broadcast exclusively on the internet by Rob Czar, a music nerd and writer, and Corinne Leigh, an environmentalist. The show is fast-paced, with a cheerfully low-budget appearance (they make it in their apartment). A substantial portion of each episode comprises video clips or still photos, or even just ideas, submitted by half a million viewers worldwide.

A couple of weeks later I got an email telling me that my clip was going to be used in the next show. When the time came, I downloaded the episode and started watching.

"Hey what's up!" said Rob. "Rob and Corinne here. Welcome to ThreadBangers."

"Recently, we received this video from John-Paul," added Corinne, getting straight to the point. And there I was, in my office, with too-long hair, twirling a couple of times to show the difference between the baggy shirt and the fitted one.

Corinne came back onscreen. "Alright John-Paul. Altering your clothes can be tricky, if you're not an experienced tailor. The easiest method we have found is pinch and pin. Take your baggy shirt, turn it inside out and put it on. Take out your pins and pinch… and pin. Once you're all pinned up you're going to sew a seam up the armpit and down the sides. Try it on and see if it fits. If you're happy, you can trim off the excess."

Not long after, another viewer sent in a video clip, in which he tested Rob and Corinne's proposal. "With my Mom's help we're going to pinch and pin each side, and see if we can get it to fit nicer." (Cut. Sound effect: Ping!) "It works! You can see how nice the sleeves fit now, and tight on my sides. Perfect!"

In the first instance, Threadbangers appealed to me because interactive web TV is essentially a great new toy: an opportunity to muck about instead of work. But the geek appeal gradually diminished. Instead, I became obsessed with the idea of fixing my shirt. It gradually dawned on me, after sending that film to ThreadBangers, that in my world it's easier to make a film than to clothe oneself – an essential second only to eating.

I decided that, in my effort to "make a difference" and "change the world", I should concentrate on this strangely overlooked necessity. But how?

chapter 21

Home-made is best – usually

Last Christmas, my friend Narmin knitted me a scarf. Having only shortly beforehand decided that I was going to knit my own jumper, and gasped after about ten rows that I would never get it done, I knew how long this must have taken her. I felt, frankly, rather overwhelmed: she could so much more easily have gone out and bought me one.

Or could she?

Ralph Borsodi, an economic theorist, decided to research the economics of home-made goods in the early 20th century - with results that astonished him.

By his own account, the idea arose in 1920, when Mrs Borsodi set about canning and preserving fruits and vegetables for winter use.

"It's great," he said, "but does it really pay?"

"Of course it does," was her reply.

Over a period of several days and nights, they set about calculating the costs involved, and comparing them with commercial production. It wasn't easy, because quite naturally they'd kept no record of how many minutes they devoted to, say, their row of tomato plants. In the event they abandoned the effort to determine gardening costs and labour costs and substituted the market value for raw materials and labour. "We did finally come to figures which I felt we might use," he wrote later. "The cost of the home-made product was between 20 per cent and 30 per cent lower than the price of factory-made merchandise.

"How was it possible, I kept asking myself, for a woman working all alone to produce canned goods at a lower cost than could the Campbell Soup Company with its fine division of labour, its efficient management, its labour-saving machinery, its quantity buying, its mass-production economies? Unless there was a mistake in our calculations, this experiment knocked all the elaborate theories framed by economists… into a cocked hat."

What economists had overlooked – he eventually concluded – was that while production costs in factories had decreased, year after year, distribution costs had increased. Indeed, he came up with an economic law: *Distribution costs tend to move in inverse relationship to production costs.*

This was not just a fanciful theory, but had a rational explanation: "With factory production, large quantities of one product are made in one spot. To use automatic machinery, to divide labour most efficiently, to transport raw materials inexpensively, it is necessary to manufacture in quantity. Raw materials and fuel must therefore be assembled from long distances before the process of fabrication can begin. After the raw materials have been fabricated into finished goods – a process which may require movement of the semi-manufactured goods back and forth among several plants located at different points across the country – the finished goods must be transported and stored at the points of consumption until the public is ready to use them. The larger factories are made in order to lower production costs, the greater become the distances, and the more intricate the problems involved in assembling the raw materials and distributing the finished goods. Thus, the lower we make the factory costs, the higher become the distribution costs."

The orthodox economic teachings to which Borsodi had previously subscribed appeared to be worthless. And by his calculations more than two-thirds of the things the average family buys could be produced more economically at home than they could be bought factory-made. So he set about bring production back into the home.

And that included clothes-making. (Though I would like to point out at this stage that I do not believe that Narmin knitted my scarf because it would be cheaper, after all, than buying one.)

The Borsodis installed a loom in their home, capable of handling fabrics up to 44 inches wide. "With such a loom, even an average weaver can produce a yard of cloth an hour. A speedy weaver, willing to exert himself, can produce thirty yards per day.

Since it takes only seven yards of 27-inch cloth to make a three-piece suit for a man, it is possible to weave the cloth for a suit in a single day on a small loom, and in less than a day on a loom able to handle 54-inch cloth."

But what particularly thrilled Borsodi, he said, was not the speed and economic value of domestic production – it was the outlet for sheer creativity.

He was by no means the first person to notice that the industrial revolution destroyed, or certainly reduced, people's capacity to be fulfilled by their work. You may be surprised to learn that Adam Smith himself identified this danger.

In the first sentence of *An Inquiry into the Nature and Causes of the Wealth of Nations*, Smith declared that the division of labour – the specialisation and concentration of workers on single subtasks – often leads to greater skill and greater productivity than would be achieved by the same number of workers each carrying out the original broad task.

His example was the making of pins.

The division of labour, Smith argued, was a great blessing – and most people still see it that way. But Smith was aware of the downside: a little further into *Wealth of Nations* he acknowledged that the division of labour leads to a "mental mutilation" in workers.

What that mutilation might involve was spelled out by another economist, EF Schumacher, in his book *Small is Beautiful*. The division of labour as generally practiced, Schumacher wrote in 1973, was not the ordinary specialisation that mankind has practiced from time immemorial but the dividing up of every complete process of production into minute parts, so that the final product can be produced at great speed "without anyone having had to contribute more than a totally insignificant and, in most cases, unskilled movement of his limbs".

In a chapter called "Buddhist Economics", Schumacher argued that to organise work in such a manner that it becomes meaningless, boring, stultifying or nerve-racking for the worker would be little short of criminal; "it would indicate a greater concern with goods than with people". And to justify it by saying that it makes time for leisure would be a complete misunderstanding of one of the basic truths of human existence: "Work properly conducted in conditions of human dignity and freedom, blesses those who do it and equally their products. If a man has no chance of obtaining work he is in a desperate position, not simply because he lacks an income but because he lacks this nourishing and enlivening factor of disciplined work, which nothing can replace."

Schumacher wasn't the first to make this case. The Victorian essayist John Ruskin responded to Smith's division of labour thus: "We have much studied and much perfected... the division of labour," he wrote. "Only we give it a false name. It is not, truly speaking, the labour that is divided but the men – divided into mere segments of men, broken into small fragments and crumbs of life – so that all the little piece of intelligence that is left in a man is not enough to make a pin, or a nail, but exhausts itself in making the point of a pin or the head of a nail."

It is a good and desirable thing, Ruskin conceded, to make many pins in a day. "But if we could only see with what crystal sand their points were polished – sand of human soul, much to be magnified before it can be discerned for what it is – we should think there might be some loss in it also."

As Ruskin saw it, the industrial revolution turned workers into drones. Leaving aside the mass production of pins, Ruskin considered architecture. The great hallmark of Gothic architecture was the freedom of the craftsmen who created it. Greek temples, by contrast, were built by slaves – "not craftsmen but human tools and machines".

Classical architecture has a pristine perfection, he said, that is artificial and mechanistic and shows no stamp of individual artists. "This desire for a pristine perfection and uniformity is, in fact, a suppression of nature and individuality."

Ruskin urges us to go out and gaze up at an old cathedral front and examine the ugly goblins, formless monsters and stern statues. "They are signs of the life and liberty of every workman who struck the stone."

One man deeply influenced by Ruskin was Gandhi, who read Ruskin's *Unto this Last* on a train. He later wrote: "I could not get any sleep that night. I was determined to change my life in accordance with the ideals of the book."

From Ruskin, Gandhi learnt that the good of the individual is contained in the good of all; that the lawyer's work has the same value as the barber's (all have the same right to earn their livelihood); and that the life of labour, as a tiller of soil or handicraftsman, is the life worth living.

Of these he said: "The first I knew, the second I had dimly realised. The third had never occurred to me."

Speaking for myself, I hadn't previously considered that mass production saps the vital creative spirit of stone masons, any more than I'd thought it did that to factory workers turning out endless quantities of identical shirts and trousers – but from now on I shall keep it in mind.

And though I know it would embarrass my younger self, I shall always henceforth prefer something hand-made to something manufactured – even, or perhaps especially, when the home-made things have obvious flaws.

Well, nearly always. There are limits to my enthusiasm for hand-made items – as evidenced by my adverse reaction to certain cheap, plasticky wristbands hawked around by an alarming woman I encountered recently in my dentist's waiting room.

Plainly, she wasn't interested in craftsmanship as such. Having put together a small number of these ghastly accessories, she told her captive audience of fellow patients that she was thinking about getting a website, and a business card. She wondered what we thought about a name she'd come up with: Beads 'r' Us.

Nobody spoke.

I wished that I was carrying a copy of Ruskin with me, so that I could read to this woman the passage indicating that, when people can find no pleasure in the work by which they make their bread, when they feel that the labour to which they are condemned is verily a degrading one, they look to wealth as the only means of pleasure.

I'd have told her that our most important task is to consider of what kinds of labour are good for us, raise us up and make us happy; and to forego such convenience, or beauty, or cheapness as is to be got only by the degradation of the workman.

It's perhaps just as well that I didn't have the book to hand.

chapter 22

Massive retail industry

Of course, there are still a few people who know how to make clothes, and they have most of us under their spell: the fashion designers.

I once spent a few days with various designers in the run-up to London Fashion Week. There was something uniformly joyless about the experience.

At studios scattered across London, cutters snipped frenetically and seamstresses stitched like surgeons – as if lives depended on their swift needlework. And 50 or so designers paced anxiously; asking themselves, in effect, if this season they had managed to come up with the goods.

The market for designer clothes in Britain is too small to sustain any single designer's career, so international sales are crucial – and the best way to generate those sales is to show your new collection on the catwalks. In a smart Marylebone townhouse, Ronit Zilkha's team worked against the tightest deadline: her show would open Fashion Week at 10.30am on the Sunday. In a yellow-painted office suite in less-fashionable Parson's Green, identical twins Tamara and Natasha Surguladze – working together as Tata-Naka – prepared for their first appearance on the Fashion Week schedule at 3.45pm on Wednesday. (They had shown before, but only "off-schedule" – unofficially, like performing at Edinburgh on the fringe, but attracted attention by scheduling their show to coincide with the least successful of the official shows – confirmation, if any were needed, that fashion is ruthlessly Darwinian.) And on two floors above a shop in North Kensington, the team behind one of London's most feted designers, Julien Macdonald, put the finishing touches to a collection that would be the last to appear in the official London Fashion Week tent. I was cautioned by Macdonald's otherwise professional PR that if I revealed anything of what I saw in the workshop he would kill me.

At the start of February, much of the preparation for Fashion Week was still unfinished. Designers and their PR teams had yet to compile final invitation lists, let alone draw up seating plans: Modus, which represents more designers than any other PR agency, had called in a dozen fashion students to stuff envelopes, while account managers wrestled with the delicate issue of who would sit where.

(Typically, the press occupies one side of the catwalk, buyers the other. In each case, the most important guests sit in the middle of the front row. At one end of the catwalk they're liable to be disturbed by the jostling of photographers; at the other, closest to the backstage area, they'll only get a good look at the outfits as the models walk back – a faintly humbling experience, akin to getting a joke only after everybody else has stopped laughing. So the question facing PRs was this: whom can we afford to offend?)

Of the four fashion capitals, London is often dismissed as the least significant. Its official show schedule, for instance, is the smallest: just 50 shows, compared with twice as many in Paris and three times as many in New York and Milan. More importantly, London has less financial clout – few designers have substantial businesses behind them – which helps to explain why so many British designers, at a certain point in their careers, are willing to be snapped up to lead the design teams at big labels overseas.

But during recent years London Fashion Week had grown steadily, attracting increasing attention from buyers and press, insists the British Fashion Council, run by John Wilson, a cheerful fellow with grey hair who by his own admission dresses less fashionably than he might, and speaks through a haze of cigar smoke in his Portland Place office.

"The new ideas you see going down the catwalk flow through into the high street," he says, by way of putting Fashion Week into context. "You have a massive retail industry depending on this."

Perhaps *too* massive. Worldwide, we spend more than $1 trillion a year on clothes. Individually, in Britain we spend around £600, on average. And we dispose of £400 worth – altogether an astounding 900,000 tons of clothing rubbish each year in the UK.

Traid is a charity that was formed in 1999 by people worried that so many clothes were sent to landfill. Traid collects second-hand clothes – a relatively tiny 3,500 tons a year – and resells them through its chain of second-hand shops in London and the south east.

I visited its warehouse in Wembley and watched workers and volunteers sort incoming donations. The man at the bottom of the conveyor wore sturdy gloves and a face mask as he ripped open bin bags that have been known to contain sex toys, grass clippings and dead cats.

Further up the line, three women sorted frantically through donations by type (trousers, shirts) and by season (winter clothes are stored during summer and vice versa). The clothes are hurled into vast cages to be re-examined by "fine sorters", some of them fashion students working as volunteers, who look more closely for problems such as tearing or stains, and subdivide the garments into two broad types, representing either upmarket chains such as Oasis and Warehouse or the less elevated Primark and Matelan. Traid's Holloway branch, catering to large numbers of students, specialises in downmarket material. Harrow takes the fancy stuff. Additionally, younger trends go to Brixton, or Brighton, while vintage clothes sell well in Notting Hill. Kilburn gets most of the saris.

Anything deemed unsatisfactory is thrown into another pool, comprising fabrics to be resold to rag traders. (It might become something else entirely, for use in gardening, hydroponics, air filtration, automotive parts, composites, bio-composites, and insulation.)

Some will end up as charitable donations to Eastern Europe or Africa.

Joe Turner of the Freedom Clothing Project points out that this is by no means a good thing, because the sheer quantity of free clothing dumped on these countries destroys the market for local clothing. If you ever wondered why rioting Africans in far-flung villages all seem to be wearing Gap sweat shirts, it's because the local clothing industry has been destroyed. Over time, as people

Zac tirelessly dabs ice-cream onto the author's washable suit.
(© Charlie Bibby, FT)

Sweatshop worker Lilia Luna and her daughter: "How come these jackets are so expensive but we get paid so little?"
(© Gautier Deblonde)

Asha Sarella, to whom the author outsourced his life.

Paul Boggia of Rentokil comes to get rid of rats. (© Dwayne Senior)

The author spreads his message on soap box in Brighton. "Don't wait! Use your politicians properly! Use them now!"
(© Simon Roberts)

Nancy in dress made of old baby grows, and decorated with pen.

Time on your hands: fabric watch made out of old scraps.

Apprenticed at Savile Row, measuring up Prince Charles's personal tailor. (© Julian Andrews)

Ancient treadle-powered sewing machine, rescued from landfill.

Author models own shirt.

With nephew Reuben wearing hat made by author using plastic bags.

Family of bears, made by the author to his own design, using various British wool yarns.

Shoes made by Nancy using cabbage leaves.

Being The Change with a spot of street-corner crochet.

Spreading the gospel in
Oxford Street.
(© Dwayne Senior)

Thich Nhat Hanh, the
Vietnamese Zen monk
who taught the author
to enjoy (among other
things) washing up.

in Africa and elsewhere forget how to make clothes, they become dependent on cheap imports – just like us.

Gandhi recognised something like this effect in India many decades ago. Under British rule, India had become dependent on British mills to spin and weave its own cotton.

As leader of the independence movement, Gandhi gave up wearing Western-style clothing and adopted the practice of weaving his own clothes from thread he'd spun himself. He encouraged others to do the same. Initially, he was disregarded or laughed at, and you can imagine why: having invented a spinning wheel all of his own, he routinely took it with him to political meetings.

But Gandhi rightly predicted that if Indians made their own clothes, it would deal a devastating blow to the British establishment in India. Within a few years, the cotton mills in Lancashire – where many of my Flintoff forebears spun Indian cotton for export back to India – had closed. And when India achieved independence Gandhi's insight was acknowledged by the addition of the spinning wheel into the national flag.

Gandhi's idea was revolutionary because it showed that a whole country's destiny can be determined by individuals doing something very small indeed – something to bear in mind next time somebody tells you that "there's no point" doing something small when the problems facing us are so big.

A small number of items sent to Traid, happily, are repaired or entirely reconfigured, to be sold under Traid's own label, Traid Remade.

"We use a lot of old T-shirts and men's shirts, and retro curtains," explains Tracey Cliffe, who runs that work. "And we use a lot of retro patterns. But I try to make them more modern, because women in the past they had tinier waists. It's nice because I get to be creative. Each piece is completely different."

Among other things, profits from the shops go into Traid's educational programme. This is run by Lyla Patel, a lively young woman whose own wardrobe is largely sourced from the warehouse. She talks to schools about landfill, climate change, wasted resources such as water used for growing cotton, pesticides, and other consequences of "fast fashion" such as sweat shops.

This does not immediately reconcile all school children to the idea of wearing second-hand clothes.

"The children will tend to say that second-hand clothes are smelly. So I say, 'Don't you have a washing machine?' And I point out that even new clothes might have been tried on many times in changing rooms. Or they say, 'I'm not poor, I don't need second-hand,' so I point out that second-hand clothes can be more expensive than new ones at Primark."

At the end of each event, children do customising workshops using trimmings and fabrics from Traid, then model their clothes on improvised catwalks. At one school in Enfield recently, 120 eleven and twelve-year-olds did this with great enthusiasm. Even the boys. "A lot of the boys use a lot of trimmings," says Madeleine Bates, Traid's PR manager, who was there with Patel. "You would expect them to think that's a bit sissy, but not at all. One boy did this amazing T-shirt which was designed to tell a girl called Abby that he loved her." Was Abby impressed? "She loved it."

To further raise awareness beyond the usual charity shop crowd, Traid recently held a massive clothes swap at a boutique in Knightsbridge, in partnership with Visa. It was open for four weeks, and people donated clothes and got credits according to what they donated. "There was a huge swap, with queues outside from 3am," says Bates. "People were rushing to buy things like Peaches Geldof's trilby and Misha Barton's bag."

Similar events are taking place all over the country. Style Swaps in Cardiff and across south Wales have raised money for Childline, and been featured in Cosmo, In Style and Elle, explains one of the organisers, Tanya Higson. "We also run auctions with ladies well, not fighting exactly, but all very much wanting the same special items."

A group called Little Vintage aims to recycle good quality children's clothes at bring-and-buy sales. The founder, Fiona Cartwright, prefers to describe the goods as "gently worn", rather than second-hand. "We have clothes ranging from Mini Boden to Baby Dior and Ralph Lauren."

As well as clothes changing hands, many people are learning once again to repair, customise and make clothes from scratch. Leah Hobson at Barnard Castle YMCA, coordinated a project in which young people made things to sell in the YMCA shop. The materials and machines were donated. "We want to encourage the young people to do something, to make and create products for sale that are recycled and therefore benefit the environment, but also earn revenue, meaning we are more sustainable and less reliant on grant funding."

Liberty, the department store, put on a show called Trash Luxe. "The backlash against the rampant consumerism of recent years has started," the store rather startlingly explained. "Sophisticated consumers are starting to value objects that have story behind them. At the same time, concern about the environment has caused many young designers to explore a "make-do and mend" approach, with the idea of appropriating existing objects and new materials and giving them new life."

The actress Helena Bonham Carter, who has always given friends hand-made presents for birthdays and Christmas ("whether they like it or not") has teamed up with her friend, the swimwear designer Samantha Sage, to produce customised clothes under the label Pantaloonies, available from Harrods. Bonham Carter has frequently been derided for her eccentric fashion sense. After a 1985 Oscars appearance she explained that at the last minute she had pulled a Miss Selfridge dress from the cupboard, worn it over a skirt of her mother's and tied a bow in the front. But that same spirit of inventive fun is what draws customers to Pantaloonies. A significant part of the fee goes to Unicef, but the last thing Bonham Carter wishes is for the enterprise to come across as "ghastly and serious". It's got to be fun, she insists.

Indeed, a young designer in London, Holly Berry, tells me she's been asked to do customising workshops at hen nights and parties.

It seems that a quiet revolution is taking place. Could this explain why high-street fashion chains have done so badly recently? Analysts typically blame poor sales figures on competition from sporting events, or bad weather. This year they blamed "interest rates starting to bite", but Rupert Eastell, head of retail at BDO Stoy Hayward, writing in Retail Week recently, acknowledged that, "This doesn't explain the strong sales increases in non-fashion sectors." Have they missed a large part of the explanation? Have they overlooked the DIY clothing revolution?

chapter 23

Down with exploitation!

I was carried away by my reading of Borsodi, Ruskin and
Schumacher, and passionately wanted them to be right.

But I was troubled by doubts.

In particular, I was troubled by Borsodi's argument that home-
made is cheaper than factory-produced goods. It simply didn't
appear to be true: it was inconceivable that anybody working at
home and knitting a jumper, for example, or weaving fabric even
on the widest possible domestic loom, could produce garments as
cheaply as the high-street chains.

The all-too obvious explanation gradually dawned on me:
it's impossible to get something cheap without somebody, or
something, being exploited.

But when I happened casually to expound my theory to
somebody I know and respect, he rejected it.

"That's not true."

The person in question has a degree from one of the world's
leading business schools, which could mean either that he knows
what he's talking about or else that he's been trained up in exactly
the kind of half-baked, self-serving economic theories that Borsodi
once mistakenly subscribed to.

I should have pointed out that by trading internationally in
things, such as clothes, that we could have produced ourselves
we are exploiting – wasting – natural resources, particularly fuel,
which isn't going to last all that much longer. (Can you imagine
somebody saying, before oil was discovered – or indeed after it has
run out, whenever that may be – that it's a sensible idea to get
British clothes made in India, or China?)

Instead, I said that I thought the international clothes trade systematically exploited people: "We export the work to India, or China, because we think it's OK to pay people there less than we would pay our neighbours, or our families, for the same work," I offered rather earnestly.

He didn't miss a beat. "There's nothing wrong with that. It's right to pay the market price for labour in those countries."

I was stumped: this struck me as both heartless and correct. But afterwards, when I'd got home, I concluded that it was only heartless.

Why? Because the market price for labour in countries such as India is distorted, and unjust. I knew this because I'd recently read the memoirs of Wangari Maathai, the Kenyan woman who won the Nobel Peace Prize in 2004.

Before the British came to Kenya, Maathai wrote, Kenyans used animals, particularly goats, as currency. The British did not want to be paid in goats but cash, and also wanted to create a workforce. So they – we – introduced an income tax for men in most parts of the country that could only be paid in cash. This immediately created a cash-based economy, and the colonial government and British settlers were the only ones with money in their hands. So Kenyans were indirectly forced to work on settlers' farms or migrate to cities to work in offices, to earn money to pay taxes. And you can be sure that they weren't paid the same rates as English workers doing similar jobs in England.

By the time Kenya won independence, its economy had come to depend on international trade in currencies that Kenyans don't control – so Kenyan labour remains cheap. The same applies to India.

So it seems to me that by paying the market rate for labour in India I can only perpetuate the injustice. And I'm sorry to conclude that I did exactly that by outsourcing my life to Asha and her colleagues. It didn't occur to me at the time, of course, but there couldn't be any other explanation: I could boss Asha around, and commission her to buy my underpants, only because the price for her labour, in India, is considerably below the price for mine, in England.

Trying to imagine how I'd have felt if our places were reversed, I cringed. Sure, it was done as entertainment, and I was always polite rather than actually bossy, but I have to say, looking back, I'm enormously grateful that she doesn't seem to hold it against me.

chapter 24

On the declining quality of underpants

I was feeling pretty dismal about all the exploitation I'd been involved in – throwing away perfectly decent clothes, taking advantage of Asha, that kind of thing.

So it came as a relatively pleasant surprise to find that the people hurt by consumerism included consumers themselves.

The reason for this is our overwhelming obsession with price, which puts downward pressure on the quality of all kinds of products, not only clothes.

Take bread: Andrew Whitley of the Village Bakery in Cumbria says there's increasing evidence that changes in wheat varieties, milling methods and baking technology have made industrial bread unpalatable – possibly even indigestible – for significant numbers of people. Why? Because of the pressure on price.

At Tesco, prices have fallen across the board by almost 30% in real terms since 1997, the company claims, saving the typical household £4,954 on its annual shopping bills. Which for many must be a blessing.

But what if prices are being depressed too much? Is that even possible? It is, thanks to websites such as mysupermarket.co.uk, which compares prices at four different online supermarkets. As you shop, the site checks your trolley to see whether there are similar but cheaper products available and even enables you to switch trolleys to a different supermarket if the price is lower for the same products.

Under pressure like that, nobody can blame supermarkets for pushing prices down and squeezing suppliers. But is the relentless pressure on price really helpful, even to consumers? Not entirely, because after increasing efficiency and economies of scale, the pressure of bargain hunters leads to the exploitation of producers – from sweatshop workers to battery chickens – and finally a decline in the quality of the goods.

Molly Scott Cato is an economist and the author of the brilliantly provocative book Market, Schmarket. She argues that the economic system elevates profit to the exclusion of all else, including quality.

"There was a time when Marks & Spencer just made good knickers and you could always buy them there. They may have been a little more expensive but the extra was worth paying because the knickers were comfortable and lasted. In the underwear department these are important considerations. But I challenge you to find a decent pair of underwear in today's high street."

Jeremy Paxman, the notoriously severe television interviewer, said much the same in an email to Sir Stuart Rose, chief executive at Marks & Spencer, that was subsequently leaked.

"I've noticed that something very troubling has happened," Paxman wrote. "[M&S] pants no longer provide adequate support. The other thing is socks. Even among those of us who clip our toenails very rigorously they appear to be wearing out much more quickly on the big toe."

Neoclassical economics, says Scott Cato, would suggest that there is a market opportunity here for somebody who produced decent underwear: "I would certainly pay a premium price. But instead all suppliers of these items are competing on price, out-sourcing production and using only the cheapest materials, so that knickers are see-through and fall apart within months.

"This is the way the best profits are made and the best knickers are no longer of any concern."

Mercifully, some persist in producing high-quality products. One is Cadolle, the French lingerie company that was instrumental in creating the first-ever bra. A couple of years ago, Harriet spent a fortune on a fitted bra from Cadolle; gratifyingly, she declared herself very pleased with it, and I subsequently coughed up for a second one for her birthday.

Another such company is Howies. Browsing idly for men's underpants on its website I was astounded to find a pair selling for

£35. That's right: £35 for a single pair. I telephoned the company to ask how it could justify the high price, and was informed that merino wool is very expensive stuff, and Howies's supplier produces it without docking the tails of the sheep – a process regarded by many as cruel.

"We don't make a lot of money on the merino," a spokeswoman confided. But she added that a well-made product will last much longer than an inferior product, and will in its lifetime have consumed fewer valuable resources.

All the same: £35 pounds for woolly pants? I weighed up for quite some time just how caring I could afford to be.

Then I thought of the poor sheep whose tails are savagely snipped off by other underwear manufacturers, considered with gratitude that I had yet to be hit by the worst of the global economic downturn – and handed over my credit card details.

chapter 25

In the spirit of Make Do And Mend, the author buys a treadle-powered sewing machine, guaranteed to work even when the lights go out

So I was becoming a better consumer, but was there anything I could do myself? *Make Do And Mend: Keeping Family and Home Afloat on War Rations* is a collection of Second World War pamphlets largely addressed to housewives. Since finding a copy of the book in the shop attached to a stately home run by the National Trust, I have darned three shirts, two pairs of jeans, a sweater, two pairs of socks and Harriet's first handmade-in-Paris bra.

My needlework is not invisible, but that's partly deliberate: I'm proud of my stitching, and don't mind if people see that I'm giving new life to clothes that, a few years ago, I would have chucked out. In fact, I nervously predict that home-darned clothing will soon be considered chic.

In this, I'm reassured by a colleague, no slouch when it comes to extravagance, who has embraced the new thrift with vim because she believes it can be "both fun and glamorous".

"I think it is chic to have darned your own clothes," India Knight told me kindly. "Darned jeans, and the fact that your winter coat is clearly something tarted up from Oxfam, definitely have cachet."

At the private nursery where Knight sends her daughter, she has noticed much less bling on display than hitherto. And she notes that in nearby shops in Primrose Hill, North London, the most expensive lotions and potions are now packaged to look bashed-up and wonky. "You pay a premium for that."

If commercial products are pretending to look home-made, no wonder making people presents is no longer a cringe-making faux pas: "Last year," Knight says joyfully, "a friend knitted me a beautiful scarf with a label saying, 'Made for you with love by Alison'. This is all about nice thrift. It can be time-consuming, but it's completely non-ironic."

Another who gave me confidence that I was doing the right thing was Vivienne Westwood. At a recent fashion show she urged people to make garments out of curtains.

"We are in the most terrible danger," she said. "In 100 years five billion people could be dead, London could be inundated in 20 years. Time is running out."

"Don't buy my clothes. Well, if you are rich or can afford a stylist, you can get me. But if not, do it yourself. My idea is that you can mix charity, vintage, Portobello Road, pieces of fabric; wrap it all around yourself, use a handkerchief as knickers, mix safety pins and jewellery. But above all do something! Be optimistic!"

Then there was Alexis Rowell, a former BBC journalist who reported for the Today programme and Newsnight before taking a business degree and working for several years in sales for technology companies. He gave all that up to do an MSc in food policy, train as an energy efficiency inspector, and stand successfully as a Liberal Democrat councillor in Camden, north London. "I had an epiphany two and a half years ago and decided to change my world. And then decided to change everyone else's lives too."

As Camden's official eco-champion, Rowell helped to organise the Camden Green Fair in Regent's Park.

"I was given the fashion workshop tent to run, which is all about making new clothes out of old ones. I thought, what would be a really good way to highlight that?" His mother had a suggestion. "She had grown up with a treadle machine – which doesn't use electricity. She found one on eBay and bought it for me from somebody in Cambridge."

Rowell has only used his car twice in the last year, and one of those trips was to pick up the sewing machine. "They thought I was crazy, 'Why don't you buy a proper sewing machine, or get yourself a girlfriend who can sew?'"

The tent was open from midday till 7pm. "It was a great day. We had a lot of kids and adults, a surprising number of men. There was one guy who came in with his girlfriend, very sceptical at first, but he came out wearing a T-shirt with fur trim. How cool is that!"

Meeting Rowell at his flat, I was taken at once to see what looked like a smart wooden side table. He flipped the top off and opened it up to reveal the beautifully painted Singer machine inside. "My pride and joy," he said, but undermined that a little by adding that he didn't use it much. His partner Laura, whom I'd yet to lay eyes on, shouted out from the bedroom that she used it all the time to mend his underpants. I realised, not absolutely immediately, that she was joking.

Then Rowell showed me some clothes he'd adapted, including a pair of trousers that had shrunk in the wash and needed letting out, and a T-shirt he'd patched to hide an ugly brand logo.

I was impressed, not least because – I can't ignore the question forever – Rowell is a man.

Taking Rowell's example, I logged onto eBay and watched several treadle-powered sewing machines fail to sell at auction. I sent a message to one disappointed seller asking if he might like to do a deal. He leaped at the chance, offering the machine for just £5, or £8 if I wanted all the bits and pieces too.

I drove to Hertfordshire and collected the machine, which had belonged to the seller's elderly and infirm mother. They didn't have room for it any more. The family had been miserable about the idea that it was going to be dumped. "We are so thrilled it's gone to a good home."

Back home, I set the machine up in my sitting room, read the ancient handbook, experimented with the treadle and applied oil to the squeaking parts. But now what?

The question was answered by a bloke who happened to come to dinner two days after I collected the machine.

I'd never met Adam before. His girlfriend is a friend of my wife. All I knew was that he teaches art at a local comprehensive. But it turned out that he also teaches textiles, and when he saw my machine he immediately offered to thread it for me. In fact, we were still mucking about with it when the others finished their soup.

Over dinner, Adam revealed that he gets virtually all his clothes from second-hand shops, and customises anything: shirts, trousers, suits. He recently made a hat for himself, and when a man stopped him on the street to ask where he got it, he made another for him, too.

I was impressed, and admitted I felt intimidated by the job of taking in my shirts – pinching and pinning as prescribed by Rob and Corinne.

"You've got to just do it," Adam advised. "Have a go. If it doesn't work, take it apart, try again. But just do it."

chapter 26

Time isn't money

Wondering how to amuse my daughter one Saturday morning, while her mother had a lie-in, I found a few scraps of material that I'd previously saved from the bin, and sewed a fabric wrist-watch.

I got the idea at Liberty, the upmarket London shop that had recently identified the backlash against rampant consumerism, but where similar handmade fabric watches cost more than £100 each.

It took a couple of hours. While I was busy, Nancy entertained herself by creating a collage using the off-cuts.

I did another for Harriet, who seemed genuinely pleased (she is perfectly happy to tell me when things aren't any good, in case I hadn't mentioned that already).

So: something genuinely fun to do, and less rubbish in the bin.

Later, in the park, they showed their watches to a friend who commented that I "obviously didn't have enough to do".

And that's just how I like it.

But I disagree when people like that friend say that making things ourselves is a waste of valuable time. Time is money, they say, but I'm not convinced. If every minute had a monetary value, how could they ever justify watching TV, or even going to bed? Surely they should be earning cash instead?

We have all been given exactly the same amount of time: precisely 24 hours a day. If we say we don't have enough time to do such and such, what we really mean is that we don't want to do it, and have allocated our time to different things instead.

I have decided to make clothes in my leisure time. Being self-employed, I decide for myself when that should be: during the day, or at night. Since I could be watching TV instead, or reading a newspaper, the time it takes to do the work is free.

You might argue that I could earn more money by writing an article or a book, and getting somebody to do my sewing for me, for less money. But there's another argument to be made: I like variety. By making my own clothes, among other things, I make my own life more varied.

I recently drew up a rather existential list of all the jobs I have done, either "for real" or as research towards an article, or just for fun. It presently reads like this: artist, baker, book-keeper, career coach, carpenter, cleaner, cook, courier, decorator, dog walker, English-language teacher, film-maker, gardener, map-maker, minicab driver, poet, police-checked child minder, potter, second-hand book seller, secretarial assistant, waiter, window-cleaner.

If you drew up a similar list, would it be as long? Or longer?

Another thing I've done for Nancy recently is darn her favourite teddy bear, Rosie. Then I sewed labels onto Rosie's outfits with phone numbers, in case she got lost. And made her a dress out of sturdy furniture fabric.

This item having satisfied Nancy, I was invited to do more along the same lines. I bought cheap off cuts of fabric and made, among other things, a dress for another favourite companion, Mrs Bunny.

Soon, I was getting nightly requests for outfits for other soft toys – and indeed for soft toys, such as a family of bears I crocheted and an elephant I knitted, and a purse, made by knitting together dozens of strings that had come with our weekly vegetable-box delivery.

Working away at these things while Nancy slept, I felt a bit like the elves who helped the shoemaker in the fairytale, only without the element of secrecy.

Then one day I found substantial quantity of unwanted clothes in a cupboard. Many items were grubby – stained in places with baby food and drool. Nobody could possibly want them at a charity shop: what to do?

I cut them into pieces, removing the grubbier parts, then stitched the pieces together. I drew blue flowers on them with a fabric marker, then attached the whole lot to the bottom of an ancient T-shirt that still, miraculously, fitted Nancy though she was coming up for five years old. Hey presto! I'd made a dress out of old rags, and it took less than two hours.

chapter 27

In which the author discovers "permaculture"

I felt tremendously pleased with myself, not only because Nancy really seemed to like the dress but because it had given me the first opportunity to put into practice the principles of "permaculture", a thrillingly upbeat response to the challenges of climate change and peak oil that I had only recently discovered.

It was brought to my attention by a man named Duncan Law, whom I visited in South London to talk about his efforts to get people growing their own food – then a rather less mainstream idea than it is now.

He took me on a tour of Brixton, stopping every so often to collect apples that had fallen from trees. (He told me about an entrepreneur who made £4,000 in the early 1950s – more than Law's headmaster father earned in a year – by commissioning children to gather blackberries for him. Law was thinking about doing something similar in south London.)

We went to see a friend of his, who had recently started growing fruit and veg in boxes in the tiny space in front of her terraced house. I still hadn't got the hang of how to be upbeat about converging global crises and ungraciously told her that the crop, though plentiful, would not be enough to keep her alive when the trouble starts.

But every lettuce you grow yourself, Law said, saves growing another one miles away and shipping it to you, and all the emissions associated with that.

Afterwards, we went back to Law's place. He showed me the incredible range of foods he grows in his not particularly big garden; and how he'd modified his loo with an item called an

Interflush, which allows him to flush exactly as much water as he might need – not too much, not too little.

Then he got out a vast pile of books about permaculture. He said I'd love it. "It will be like coming home," he promised.

I'm a sucker for inspirational promises like that. So I bought a few of Law's books from him there and then. By the time I'd crossed London on the Tube I had already acquired a pretty good grasp of permaculture – basically, a design system for creating abundance with minimum effort.

What that means, in practice, is working with nature rather than against it.

The classic example is "no dig" gardening. Why bother to dig, permaculturists ask, when worms will aerate the soil for you? If you are worried about weeds, just pop down some cardboard to deprive them of light. The cardboard will eventually rot down, and in the meantime you can make little holes in it and plant the things you do want to grow – and put your feet up instead of putting your back out.

Or you could even embrace the weeds. In permaculture – as I found after doing considerably more reading, not a small part of it in the magazine, *Permaculture*, that is published by the admirable and cheerful people who published the book you are now reading – weeds are not always reviled.

"It's how we look at things that make them advantageous or not," explains a regular contributor, Graham Burnett, in an essay called "Permaculture: A Beginner's Guide". A weed is just a plant that is growing in the wrong place, and may have many virtues that we've not yet discovered.

Dandelions, for instance, attract bees, provide flowers that can be made into delicious wine, leaves that add flavour to salad, and roots that can be roasted as a coffee substitute or eaten like carrots. (Additionally, the deep roots pull up valuable minerals from the subsoil.)

You will have gathered by now that this is a book primarily about clothes. But I hope it's obvious that many of the insights it contains, if that's not too grand a term, apply equally to other parts of life, such as food growing, and vice versa.

Thus, while many of us have grasped that it's not a brilliant idea to fly apples to the UK from New Zealand, when we can eat local, seasonal food instead, with considerably fewer carbon emissions – it's similarly nuts to import cotton from India (certainly at the rate we do) instead of using plentiful local fibres.

To put that a bit more cheerfully: if a dandelion can be regarded as a Jolly Good Thing, and odd blackberries growing here and there and generally disregarded can be transformed by an army of schoolboy pickers into a valuable resource, then it's no surprise that a heap of Nancy's grubby baby-grows can be transformed (if I say so myself) into a beautiful dress.

What was formerly regarded as a problem can itself become a solution.

chapter 28

A surprisingly manly chapter

Almost exactly a year after rats last appeared in our cellar, I was sitting in the kitchen when I heard something gnawing at the floorboards beneath me.

After talking it over with Harriet, who was understandably appalled, I telephoned Rentokil. I had been glad of the company's help last year, and was happy to get them back.

But it turned out that the fearless Paul Boggia had moved on. I wasn't sure that I wanted anybody else. Also, the company seemed determined to sign me up for a long-term, rolling contract to keep the rats under control forever.

It was going to cost a fortune, and I could see already how irritating it would be to make appointments in advance and have to stay in for them – and probably fail to do so, sometimes, if something came up at work, and miss out on the service we were paying for.

I started to go off the idea, and recognised an opportunity to put into practice my new theory that I should do (virtually) everything myself unless there was a very compelling reason not to.

Harriet wasn't sure. She said she didn't want me to get bitten, but I suspect that she also didn't think I was up to doing the job properly.

So I started work while she was out of the house – keeping the operation secret, like Danny Wallace hiding Join Me from his girlfriend.

I pulled up a couple of floorboards near the front door, put on my toughest shoes and a torch that fitted to my forehead, and placed a loud radio on the floor beside me. Then I lowered myself between the close-fitting joists and hoped that no rat would attack my dangling legs.

The space below the floor smelled of damp and, obviously, of rats. As I moved, the torch threw alarming shadows off the various brick columns holding up the joists. I whistled as loudly as I could, scanning wide-eyed for rodents. But after a while it became clear that, even if they were down there with me, they were hiding.

So I took my time, and searched every corner to find where they were coming in and out. Eventually I found among the dusty old bricks a tiny hole with a suspicious number of droppings nearby.

I climbed back out, dusted myself down, and went to buy three traps. If I had to kill sentient-beings (copyright: the Buddha) I would rather not be responsible for slow and painful death by poison. And rather than fill the traps with chocolate, which I've seen rats snaffle without harm, I smeared sticky peanut butter on them. Nasty, eh?

Back down into the dark I went, and left the traps in three corners, didn't even attempt to seal the entry point, and left.

The next day, I went back down again, and found a dead rat in one of the traps. I scooped him up, or possibly her, and popped the carcass into a carrier bag, then reset the trap.

Over the days that followed, I went down again and again. There was little sign of activity, so I tried filling the hole in the wall – wedging pieces of brick as far in as I could manage, then wire wool, and finally the unpleasantly sticky expanding foam that Paul Boggia had used.

I could only hope the rats were not getting in and out beneath the kitchen floor, too, because I couldn't get underneath that part, and really didn't want to take the floor up.

Two days later, to my great dismay, I heard rats again. But this time I didn't merely fret: I took action. I practically dived through the joists and found that the rats had bulldozed through the hole I'd filled. So I did it again, only this time I made it even more secure. And before leaving, I reset the traps, because if a rat was trapped down there it might try to chew its way out – much better (for us, anyway) if it left by way of the trap, and one of my plastic-bag shrouds.

Over the following weeks, as and when the mood grabbed me, I popped down into the cellar to check things out. It has been nearly a year now, and I've not heard or seen anything.

Harriet agreed that I was right to take matters in hand myself: I had indeed saved money. But more important, from my point of view, was the powerful feeling of responsibility and capability that I'd never have felt if I'd got in the experts.

The feeling turned out to be addictive.

We'd been piling up books recently and urgently needed to build new shelves. Harriet got a carpenter round to measure up and give us a quote for a fitted bookcase on the landing outside my office, but for weeks on end after he came, we heard nothing.

Now, he's a very good carpenter and a nice chap, but I didn't relish paying what was bound to be a high price, and I reckoned I could build what we needed myself.

Naturally, I didn't tell Harriet, at this stage.

Instead, as I'd done with the rats, I started work as soon as she'd left home in the morning. I grabbed my tape measure and pencil and drew a sketch of what was required. Then I went to a hardware shop round the corner and bought £20 of timber from managed forests. To minimise my environmental impact, I decided to use dowel to join the wooden parts, rather than metal screws.

By lunchtime, I'd cut the wood by hand into the right sized pieces and drilled holes for the dowels. Not very long afterwards, the shelves were finished. I used two small metal braces to fix them to the wall, then filled the shelves with books and took care to show them to Nancy first.

"Wow!" she said, very generously. "That's amazing, Daddy!" This was a great help, because it meant that when Harriet came home I would already have Nancy on my side – but as it happens that was unnecessary because even Harriet was impressed.

And so ends what I hope you will agree was a refreshingly manly chapter.

chapter 29

The Young Pretenders

I had decided to make an entire outfit, but this did not necessarily mean making everything from scratch. I could also modify clothes I had already, or use second-hand clothes.

Swap-O-Rama-Rama is a clothing swap and series of do-it-yourself workshops, founded by Wendy Tremayne in 2005. Since then, it has grown to include more than 50 cities in the US and several countries around the world and it continues to grow.

Every swap begins with a giant collective pile of clothing, the unwanted clothing of all who attend – as many as 3,000 have attended individual events in the past. Everyone is welcome to dive in and find items from the pile – tragic shopping mistakes, well worn and loved items that have exceeded their stay in the cupboard, unloved gifts. It's all free: all you have to do is modify it and, if you're brave, take a playful spin down the catwalk.

"Swap-O-Rama-Rama helps people break down the barrier between consumer and creator," Tremayne tells me. "Through hands-on experience, it invites the discovery that the making of things is not an activity to be avoided in order to attain leisure, but rather a playful and leisurely endeavour unto itself."

I'm rather impressed by Tremayne, a songwriter and musician by background who last had a "job" (as she puts it) in 2000 and has since devoted herself only to projects that seemed meaningful to her – such as serving as a volunteer member of the Dali Lama's press team in New York and, in 2005, setting up that city's first unisex naked yoga class.

"We find ourselves trapped in a culture of helplessness unable to perform the simplest of tasks, such as hemming a skirt. Should we question our role in this process we are reminded that the making of things prevents us from having leisure time. But what does one do with all that leisure time? We shop!"

As Tremayne sees it, the society we live in has been 100 per cent commodified. She decided to "deconstruct" consumerism by living for a year entirely on barter. This involved setting up clothes swaps, and out of that was born Swap-O-Rama-Rama.

Quite deliberately, she puts on the events without mirrors, so that people there must turn to a stranger and ask whether a certain outfit suits them or not. Additionally, visitors are supplied with labels that say "100% modified by me".

Tremayne's insights are delivered with passion, and make a lot of sense. They're a useful reminder that making your own clothes is not only about improving the world "out there". It's also about changing ourselves, and not only in the superficial way popularised by Trinny and Susannah.

There's a historical model: Elizabeth Fry, the Quaker philanthropist who features on the £5 note.

As a young woman, Fry enjoyed fine clothes: her diary records her going to meeting for worship wearing scandalously purple boots with scarlet laces. But as she became more aware of the world around her she decided – as Gandhi did after her – to change the way she dressed. She became what was known as a "plain Friend". (This didn't go down well with her family, wealthy tea, coffee and spice merchants.)

As a plain Quaker, Fry began the work for which she is now remembered: she helped found the Association for the Improvement of the Female Prisoners in Newgate, which provided materials so that prisoners could sew, knit and make goods for sale, raising cash to buy food, clothing and fresh straw. Additionally, women transported to the colonies were provided with tools and materials to make patchwork quilts on the voyage, which could be sold on arrival to provide an income that protected many of them from becoming prostitutes.

If I hadn't thought of Fry already, I would certainly have done so when, shortly after my visit to Traid's warehouse, Lyla Patel invited me to a fashion show in Brighton, where young offenders were to model outfits they'd made out of second-hand clothes.

The event took place at The Old Ship, on the sea front. The young offenders – two male, two female – were scheduled to model their clothes immediately after the interval.

The audience comprised about 150 very well dressed customers of Brighton's smartest boutiques. When I popped out of the dressing room to see them the first time, they were considering a range of bridal outfits. The next time, they were looking at fetish clothes, and emitting raucous whoops.

In the crowded dressing room, I met a social worker, Jo Bates. "We have maybe 100 young people on our books," she told me. Typically the offences include criminal damage, theft, assault, possession of illegal drugs, public disorder. "We put out an email and these four came forward. This isn't about punishment, it's about sharing experiences and opportunities that these people might not have had before. It's about building their confidence and raising expectations.

Over the next hour or so, the four demonstrated clearly how nervous they are. "I'm going to mess up at the last minute," said one, Chelsea. Another, Connor, announced: "I'm not going on the stage. I'm not."

Patel, who has seen this kind of nerves before, told me that her greatest satisfaction, tonight, came from seeing Connor wear a shirt from Traid. "He was so anti-Traid and second-hand clothes. But I found him a Dior shirt for £6."

At 9.30, as the interval drew to a close, the four manically practiced their catwalk moves. One, Louis, wiggled about in the jacket he had customised. "I'm over the worst now," he told me. "This morning, I was shaking." Meanwhile Sadie agonised about her strapless top falling loose. The others took their places ready to step through to the catwalk. Connor, at the front, checked his lipstick. Sadie went crazy with hairspray.

Patel darted among them pulling encouraging faces as Bates took photos.

For the purposes of the show, the four took the name Young Pretenders – a pun on their legal status. But they didn't seem to have imagined that their criminal record would be mentioned. Standing just out of site behind the curtain, ready to go on, they heard the MC reveal this to the audience, to emphasise quite how much they have achieved in a short time.

"That is so snide!" said Sadie. Chelsea's mortification was interestingly different: she was upset that he told the audience their clothes are second hand.

But there was no time to indulge this fury. All at once, David Bowie's "Fashion" started up and the four strutted onto the stage. I rushed through the changing room and round the back to place myself among the audience, who were clapping and whooping enthusiastically.

It was over in no time. Bursting breathless back into the dressing room, Sadie said, "Oh, God, I look fat on the monitors! I'm shaking. I feel like crying."

One of the other models came over to say how well they had all done.

Connor said: "I want to do it again!"

"That was so good," Patel told me. "I was feeling sick beforehand." Bates agreed. "But they were the best thing in the show."

chapter 30

Fresh Air Machine

But what was I to customise?

I'd been doing a lot of cycling recently, and noticing, not for the first time, that the sight of me makes people laugh, or anyway smile. This has something to do with me being tall, and the foldaway bike having tiny wheels: I look like a clown. Harriet actually blushed when I told her that people point and laugh, but it doesn't bother me. On the contrary, I'm glad to amuse them, and generally smile back.

But I wondered if it was possible to harness all that good-humour to some useful purpose.

After giving the matter some thought, I decided to customise one of my Thomas Pink shirts with the slogan "Fresh Air Machine", in big letters on the back, so that drivers could see it as I cycled. I still admired Sian Berry's spoof parking tickets, but wondered if the customised shirt might usefully encourage drivers, rather than scold them.

It wasn't my own slogan, to be honest. When I was at primary school, my class spent two hours a week with Ivor Cutler, by then well known as a poet and musician, who didn't so much teach us as entertain us with an indescribable combination of role-play, dance and barmy made-up songs.

Mr Cutler's lessons made a very strong impression on me, and when I was first starting out as a journalist I phoned Mr Cutler and asked if he would be prepared to do an interview that I might subsequently try to sell.

He kindly consented, so I went to see him at his flat in north London. After asking questions and writing down his answers I also took photographs. And then we both relaxed. He gave me, to take away, for reasons that I no longer recall, a printed sheet of voice-training exercises and some tiny gold stickers.

Till that moment, I'd forgotten about the stickers. Mr Cutler used to give out stickers all the time at school. They were printed up with slogans, variously droll and affirmative, in tiny letters. The ones he gave me this time said simply: Fresh Air Machine. He had stuck one on his bicycle, he said, and on getting home I decided to stick one on my bike too.

Several years later, I decided to get rid of that bike. It was in good shape, but I didn't have anywhere to keep it. So I left it unchained beside a lamp post for somebody to take it away. For weeks, nothing happened. Then somebody chained it to the post. Then somebody (else, presumably) stole the wheels, the saddle and other parts. Three years later, there was only the rusty frame, still chained to the lamp post, and still bearing Mr Cutler's sticker.

Not long after seeing the bike in that rather sad condition, I learned that Mr Cutler had died. Feeling very sad, I went onto Amazon to buy CDs of his songs and poems, and laughed at the cover images. And it dawned on me that the real fresh air machine was not the bike but Mr Cutler himself. And if he could be a Fresh Air Machine, I could be one too.

chapter 31

Hiding light under a bushel

Elizabeth Fry, Gandhi, even Wendy Tremayne, the Dalai Lama's volunteer press assistant... it was becoming clearer to me that the people who had the most to teach me were often motivated by insights that they themselves might have called religious.

This fascinated me because in clever metropolitan circles the prevailing view holds, with professor Richard Dawkins and others, that religion is basically awful, oppressive and premised on lies.

I became slightly obsessed about finding the religious motivation, if that's what it was, behind anybody who inspired me.

It wasn't always affirmative. When I interviewed Harold Pinter, the Nobel-prize winning writer, about his opposition to the war in Iraq, he mentioned calling a friend in America not long after 9/11. "She wasn't there. So her answering machine came on and said: 'I am out, I'll be back at four o'clock' – or whatever it was – 'God bless America.' When I heard those words, I looked at the receiver and put it very slowly down." He didn't call her again. "God of course is on the American side. And blessing America. I find it stultifying and pathetic."

Then there was Daryl Hannah, the actress and activist who asked me, after a decorous interview over tea at her London hotel, to schlep around the city behind her, carrying a camera and a nine-foot flagpole as she filmed a story for her video blog, Daryl Hannah Love Life, and to line up on her behalf last-minute meetings with representatives of the UK's green grassroots. I was delighted – absolutely delighted – to oblige.

One person I introduced her to was Lyla Patel's partner, Richard Reynolds, king of the Guerrilla Gardeners, who kindly agreed, without any notice at all, to take us to film him at a big traffic island that he and some friends had planted up with lavender. Later, in front of Big Ben, on the river, and at Trafalgar Square, Hannah unfurled a vast white flag made of knotted carrier bags, and skipped about for the camera – very possibly in breach of anti-terror laws which have seen people arrested for holding tea parties this close to parliament.

I was particularly impressed by the flag, and wondered about the knotting technique. I was also delighted that, when Hannah asked if anybody had a piece of string to hold something together, I was able to say that I did, indeed, have some string – because Nancy had garlanded me with a "necklace" made of the string that comes with our weekly vegetable box.

Wherever we went, we took public transport – at great hazard to other passengers from the nine-foot flagpole – because Hannah is careful about how she travels. "People really have to consider lifestyle change. I have not been to a gas station since the turn of the century. And that is liberating."

I asked her at one point about her religious background: Hannah was raised a Catholic, but "flunked the catechism" and is not allowed to take communion. "I took the tenets to heart," she explained. "I asked why we couldn't take the gold from the ceiling and give it to the poor. If you ask questions that means you don't have faith. And they didn't like me colouring in the pictures in my Bible."

Another time, I spoke to a man who is absolutely adored – Rob Hopkins, creator of the Transition Town movement. There's a phrase people use, "I'll have whatever he's had," which particularly suits Hopkins: his cheerful good humour and optimism in the face of vast planetary threats is incredibly infectious. Many people, I'm sure, would be delighted to have whatever he's had.

Well, I had noticed a Tibetan name in the acknowledgements to Hopkins's book on Transition Towns. When I met him, I asked him about that. He told me the man had been a great influence on him. If that was so, I wondered why he didn't tell people about it. Why play down the Buddhism?

He looked a bit thrown by the question, then said he didn't think it would be useful. "I don't think it would help to say, in effect: 'Transition Towns, brought to you by a load of Buddhists.'"

Similarly, I had a coffee once with a public relations woman whose clients include practically every ethical business I can think of, including the people who deliver local, seasonal food to my doorstep every week and the wind-powered electricity company that ships power to my meter. I mentioned idly that my work was leading me back again and again to religion – how the ancient wisdom seemed so often to be spot-on.

Why did everybody get so embarrassed about it? I wondered aloud.

Again there was that puzzled, hesitant expression. Then she revealed that she was herself an evangelical Christian. The motive underlying everything she did was: Love Thy Neighbour as Thyself, she said, and the greatest thing she could ever do would be to bring somebody to Christ. But like Hopkins she kept it to herself, because she didn't want people to hold it against the companies she represented, and the ideas she tried to put across.

chapter 32

Living biblically

I was standing in Oxford Street. Hundreds of shoppers walked past me every minute. I tried to catch they eye of the ones who come closest. But most had perfected the art of looking right through me – because I was holding up a sign that read: "Thou Shalt Not Covet".

The tenth commandment: Thou Shalt Not Covet, is the one that most of us break most frequently. Indeed, the modern economy, which depends on constant growth, requires us to covet more or less ceaselessly. Christmas is peak coveting season – which is why I took my sign to Oxford Street, the belly of the beast.

After ten minutes, in which period my nose and fingers gradually turn to ice, I finally got a response to my biblical injunction. A man wearing a raincoat muttered through the side of his mouth as he passed close by: "Well done mate."

It wasn't much, but it helped. The life of a biblical prophet is hard and lonely. Just ask Jeremiah, who walked the streets with a yolk around his head to signify enslavement to the Babylonians. Or Isiah, who walked naked and barefoot for three years for similar reasons.

As a latter-day prophet of only a few days standing, I couldn't hope to match those two, but I took satisfaction from this stranger's muttered support.

I decided to stop bossing and prohibiting for a while, in favour of something more constructive. I put away the tenth commandment and held up instead a sign that read: "Love Thy Neighbour".

This one proved much more acceptable to the shoppers. A woman stopped in front of me and declared, "Oh, that's nice."

I hadn't given up on Christianity. On the contrary, I felt a lot more comfortable trying to follow the teachings of Christ now that I had Buddhism to fall back on.

In both traditions, it's regarded as no bad thing to be humble. Well, it takes a certain amount of humility to confess that I owed my presence in Oxford Street, once again, to the American writer A J Jacobs.

Two years after Jacobs published his story about outsourcing his life, he wrote a book about trying to live biblically. I was invited to follow up with a story on the same lines for *The Sunday Times*.

Jacobs, an agnostic, decided to devote a year of his life to living biblically – to spend 12 months trying to observe the 700 or so rules set out in the Old and New Testaments. Not just the obvious ones – the ten commandments, loving his neighbour – but also rules whose original meaning has been obscured, or which modern law has overtaken, such as the prohibition on wearing clothes made of mixed fibres.

Having completed his experiment, Jacobs published *The Year of Living Biblically*. This combines amusing accounts of his struggles to keep the more obscure rules with a surprisingly reflective and sincere expression of gratitude for the wisdom he gained – sometimes as a result of following those same rules.

For instance, Proverbs asserts that smiling makes you happy. As it turns out, psychology agrees: the theory of cognitive dissonance suggests that if you behave in a certain way, your beliefs will eventually change to conform to your behaviour. This could be taken further, Jacobs suggests: if you act like you're faithful and God loving, you might actually turn out to be.

In the week before Christmas, I decided to give it a go.

As with my previous foray into organised Christendom, I was intellectually interested. I'd become increasingly fed up, reading or listening to the atheist polemicist Professor Richard Dawkins bang on about God not existing. As he must surely know, the square root of minus one doesn't exist either, but that doesn't mean it's entirely without interest, or indeed practical use. Dawkins pretends that everybody religious is either an idiot or dangerous, or both, but it's bad science to ignore the evidence that most believers find religion a useful support in their efforts to be better, and don't wish to be suicide bombers.

But there are other reasons, as Jacobs pointed out, to follow the Bible's teachings.

Specifically, chapter 28 of Deuteronomy, says that if you don't, you shall be cursed in the city and in the field, cursed when you come in and cursed when you go out. The Lord will send vexation, make the pestilence cleave unto you, smite you with a consumption, and with the mildew. You shall not prosper. Locusts will consume the trees and fruit of your land. Your sons and daughters shall be given to another people and your eyes will fail with longing for them. You will fear day and night. You will become an astonishment, a proverb and a byword among all nations.

But what exactly does it mean to live biblically? I emailed an assortment of acquaintance for tips. Some seemed to think that avoiding modern conveniences would do the trick. "Write your emails in stone... by candlelight," wrote Rob, from Threadbangers.

Another drew up a long list of prohibitions. "No deodorants – you can spray frankincense if you get a bit whiffy. No potatoes. No underpants."

One thought it necessary to re-enact biblical behaviour. "You could try insisting that your hosts at parties wash your feet when you arrive. Might prove challenging, but worth trying."

More than a few suggested I should try to sleep in a stable. West Hampstead police station has stables. I phoned them to ask whether it might be possible to stay one night. The man who answered the phone was extremely polite but said no. Would it make a difference that the person in question promised to live biblically, so obviously wouldn't be breaking any of the ten commandments? Alas, the horses might break out, and there were health and safety requirements to observe, because of the insurance. "I understand the motivation," he said, "and you have my sympathy" – but then the line went dead. I hoped he'd not fallen into Satan's hands.

One friend, in the diplomatic service, had little to offer in the way of advice, just this rather unbiblical boast: "By the way, I ain't living biblically, I got loads of totty on me case doing the let's-try-to-seduce-the-married-bloke thing; but I am doing what the FCO does in unclear situations… nothing."

I was glad he's doing nothing, because if he committed adultery I might need to stone him.

Jacobs set out to stone adulterers in Manhattan but realised this would get him into trouble. His solution was to use very small pebbles and to drop them as if by accident on the adulterer's shoe. It didn't work. He encountered an elderly adulterer who, realising what Jacobs was up to, snatched his stones and hurled them back.

Jacobs works on *Esquire* magazine, which tends to involve working with pictures of scantily clad women. He developed several strategies for dealing with lustful thoughts. First, imagine that the object of those thoughts is simply beyond your grasp. Second, think of her as if she were your mother. ("More effective than strategy one, and more disturbing," he says.) Third, recite Bible passages to distract yourself. Fourth: do not objectify. Think of her as a complete person. Imagine her childhood, her favourite novel, whether she uses a PC or Mac.

Over the course of a year, these strategies had an unexpected effect. "I figured it would get more and more difficult to suppress my sexuality," Jacobs reports, "like water building up behind a dam. But it's more like my sex drive has evaporated."

Elsewhere, Jacobs writes of the loneliness of not being allowed to touch his own wife for a week after she's had her period. But he justifies the purity laws that forbid this. It's not misogynistic, he says, it's an expression of reverence for life – or rather, a way to respect the ending of life. "When a woman has her period, it's like a little death. A potential life has vanished."

His wife is unimpressed. On learning that he is not allowed to sit on chairs she has sat on during the seven days she's unclean, she wilfully sits on every seat in the house.

More enjoyable for Jacobs and his wife alike was his attempt to keep the Sabbath. (A "school's out for summer" feeling every week.) The strictest keepers of the Sabbath are orthodox Jews, for whom 39 different types of work are off-limits, including cooking, combing and washing. "You can't tear anything," Jacobs explains, "so toilet paper must be pre-ripped earlier in the week."

Does writing for *The Sunday Times* break the Sabbath? I hope not. My own work finishes long before Sunday – but to cover myself against other infractions I set aside half an hour to pre-rip loo paper.

Speaking biblically requires a total switch in the content of conversation: no lying, no complaining, no gossiping. (The rabbis compare gossip with murder.) For me, this is not a huge problem. I work at home, so there's nobody to lie or complain to, most of the time, or gossip about.

When it comes to swearing, I decided some time ago to say things like crikey and even cripes. This has now become second-nature, and I really feel less angry as a result. This has certainly been Jacobs' experience, since he started to say "fudge". "It sounds so folksy, so Jimmy Stewartish and amusingly dorky, that I can't help but smile. My anger recedes."

*

A few days into my experiment, I decided to spread the Gospel by showing Nancy highlights of Jesus Christ Superstar, the Andrew Lloyd Webber musical, on video.

I kept the remote close to hand: tough-minded parents might think she's old enough to watch a crucifixion, but I don't. She's scared enough when a giant snowball blocks the railway tracks on Postman Pat.

Early on, there was a crowd scene with lots of hosannas and cheerful waving of palms. "Why are they so excited about Jesus?" Nancy asked, perfectly reasonably. Alas, the hosannas were soon intercut with a song from the Pharisees which concludes: "Jesus must die."

Nancy's obsessed with death, and wanted to know how the naughty black-hat people were going to bring it about. I wished I hadn't started this. The questions were endless. "Did they make him die or was he just an old man?" No, I'm afraid he wasn't an old man, he died when he was quite young. "Is he going to die now?" No, he dies a bit later.

When Jesus smashed up the bazaar in the temple I was at a loss to explain. "It's because you're not meant to do shopping in temples," I offered lamely. "Why do you not do shopping in the temple?" Nancy asked. Silence.

Before any duffing up begins – let alone the crucifixion – I stopped the film. I told Nancy I don't want her to watch people hitting other people. The next morning her first words to Harriet are a request that they watch the Jesus film together because she wants to show her the bit where the naughty people hit Jesus. What have I done?

As penance, I sing Morning Has Broken several times, hoping I'm loud enough to bring cheer to my neighbours. Remembering school assemblies, I dig out my old treble recorder, which I've not played since I was about 10. Even without written music, I find I'm able to remember the fingering. A miracle!

Half-way through his Bible project, Jacobs came to the conclusion that he was "trying to fly solo on a route that was specifically designed for a crowd". He had missed out on the feeling of belonging, a key part of religion.

Well I had already carried out my own experiment, on that front, by sampling different Christian denominations. None had absolutely grabbed me, but I had been back to the Quakers – not just once but several times. I found the silence, and the shared ministry, very satisfying.

But like Jacobs I was baffled by the bible.

"How can the ethically advanced rules and the bizarre decrees be found in the same book?" Jacobs asks. "And not just the same book. Sometimes the same page. The prohibition against mixing wool and linen comes right after the command to love your neighbour. It's not like the Bible has a section called, 'And Now for Some Crazy Laws'."

Worried that he was devoting too much attention to the weird parts, and neglecting the goodness and justice, he took advice from a rabbi. "Try to make everything you do measure up to the moral standards of the prophets," he was told.

Hoping to do that myself, and conscious of the need to love my neighbour, I collared the vicar at my local church after the candle-lit carol service. I asked him if I could join the board of the old people's home at the end of my garden.

It was a busy week for vicars, but he promised to make the arrangements in January.

And what about prayer? I'd been avoiding this, or pretending that singing, or playing recorder, was sufficient.

Jacobs had difficulty too, initially, but gradually found himself looking forward to prayer sessions. "Prayers are moral weight training – ten minutes in which it's impossible to be self-centred."

He learned to say "God willing" whenever making a reference to the future – that is, about 80 times a day. His mother said he sounded like somebody who sends videos to Al Jazeera. "But I find it a profound reminder of the murky instability of the future."

Being somewhat obsessive compulsive, Jacobs got carried away with thanksgiving. "I'm muttering to myself, 'Thank you... thank you... thank you.' It's an odd way to live. But I've never before been so aware of the thousands of good things, the things that go right every day."

Seeking guidance on prayer, I called some of the big churches and told them I was living biblically.

Perhaps surprisingly, a spokesperson for the Roman Catholic Archbishop of Westminster failed to recommend any of the more outlandish stuff: she said nothing about foregoing deodorant, or potatoes, or underpants.

"It's not about eating locusts but looking at your heart. That is what makes you happy. You won't want to stop after a week. This gives you a deep sense of peace and happiness in the long term."

She said, gratifyingly, that advent was the perfect time to carry out my project. "We are all looking at how we lead our lives, in preparation for Christ's birth.

"The heart of the Christian life," she said, "is to love God and your neighbour." In practice, this means setting aside time to worship, say sorry for mistakes, thanks for the good stuff, and ask for help for people who need it.

"You can pray on your own or in church. You don't need to follow particular words. The heart of it is to talk to God and share what is on your mind. And listen."

What, for a voice?

"Be open to the Lord's nudging and guidance."

As for loving my neighbour, this means treating others as I would like them to treat me – the Golden Rule. Treat them with kindness and truth, particularly the poor and the suffering.

But I should not be proud in my heart and think myself better than anybody. If I do a good thing, I shouldn't boast about it. I should focus my mind on the example of Jesus Christ, and if that isn't enough I could think too of the Blessed Virgin Mary, and my namesake the late Pope John Paul. "He particularly respected the dignity of all people."

For balance, I found an Anglican website which provided a formula for prayer that uses our digits as prompts. The thumb reminds us to think of our closest friends and relations, the index finger points towards our teachers, the middle finger represents people with power, the ring finger reminds us of the powerless and the poor, and only finally with the little finger do we think of ourselves.

I had several goes at this, only rarely getting to the little finger to think of myself because I got so carried away thinking good thoughts for the teachers, and people in power.

One who came to mind most often was Richard Dawkins. I prayed for Dawkins a very great deal indeed.

Always keeping in mind the Golden Rule, I prayed to God the Father, the Son and the Holy Ghost, to the prophets, to the Blessed Virgin Mary, to my namesake the late Pope, and for good measure to the square root of minus one. I called on them all to shower blessings on the professor, and bring him a Happy Christmas – whether he likes it or not.

chapter 33

*Copying the Brooks Brothers shirt –
with help from Great Aunt Peggy*

Ever since I'd been in touch with Threadbangers, it had niggled to be told that adapting my shirt in a more than rudimentary way would be difficult. I don't know where it comes from, but deep down in me is a very strong refusal to believe that there's anything I can't do if I really want to. (This doesn't mean that I can do things superlatively, but that I can at least have a go. I fully accept that I'm not going to win a gold medal for sprinting.)

So I got out that old Brooks Brothers shirt and took it to a local fabric shop, Desai, determined to make a new one.

The young woman in the shop suggested that I'd need slightly more than two metres, and brought forward a roll of white polycotton. This cost only £1.75 a square metre, she explained. "Pure cotton is £6 a square metre – so if you make a mistake this would not be so expensive…"

This was correct, but on the other hand I would never wear the polycotton. I doubted that I had sufficient oomph to make a whole shirt that I would never wear.

She changed tack. "You might as well get good fabric. Some of the better shirts, ready made, start at £120 in the shops, and you could buy the material for £24 here."

Hm. Twenty-four pounds still seemed like quite a lot. There was every chance that I would make a hash of the whole project.

"There's another one I have," she suggested. "It's pure cotton, but some of it is marked, so we're clearing it for £2.50 a square metre. Five pounds for a shirt."

I liked this idea.

She unrolled the bolt of pale blue material and measured each metre against a wooden stick. She pointed out one of the blemishes. "They're tiny. Hopefully you can cut them out when you do the pattern."

This was going to be difficult, wasn't it?

She recommended that I take my original shirt to a nearby seamstress, where they could make me a paper pattern without taking it apart or damaging it at all.

That sounded like a very good idea. When I started making the shirt, she said, I should sew as much as I could by hand, with big, loose stitches, and when that was right go over it with the machine. "It's easy when you get the hang of it. The front and back is simple, it's the collars, and fitting the sleeves in. Once you've done one shirt... you'll be fine."

I took her advice and took the new material and my old Brooks Brothers shirt to Chinsardy, the local seamstress on Finchley Road, where the proprietor, Lucy, was happy to help. I asked her, since this was my first such project, to cut me a paper pattern from my old shirt, and to cut the material too.

I asked for tips. She showed me a model of the female form.

"You see the back, the waistline, the bust, the hip, the shoulder, the neckline, the back of the neck, across the back... whenever you do a pattern you must take all these into consideration."

I asked if she thought I was going to manage.

"How good is your sewing? A good shirt has to be neatly finished. The buttonholes have to be neat, and so on."

She recommended that I practice making a yoke, and sewing collars. "And there is something here we call a placket." This turned out to be the bit that runs up the sleeve from the cuff. "You need to learn how to fit these on. You could get some calico and practice making lots of cuffs and sleeves. Even how to do straight stitches... It's quite an intense process."

She was smiling, but this sounded bad.

"You can buy patterns on the internet. They have information with them, and instructions. But reading books is quite different from having your hands on deck."

Perhaps my choice of garment – a fitted shirt – was too ambitious?

"Have you done anything like this before?"

"I made a jacket for my daughter's teddy bear."

"So it didn't need any fitting."

"Well, it had to fit the bear."

"Then this is going to be a bit of a challenge."

A few days later I went to collect the paper pattern and the cut fabric. I took them home in a carrier bag and left it beside my desk for several weeks. I had no deadline, and frankly still found the project intimidating.

But then I heard that Harriet's great-aunt Peggy would be joining us for the Bank Holiday weekend at my in-laws' house in Somerset, and decided to start my project there. After all, Peggy's an accomplished seamstress, veteran make-do-and-mender of many items belonging to my wife, and over the years has seemed to find my projects amusing.

I was not prepared for quite how interested and involved Peggy turned out to be. It's ungallant to mention somebody's age, but it helps to understand what I mean when I say that Peggy was 97 years old at the time. She really attacked the project with vim, showing me how to knot thread quickly, using just one hand, and practically barking instructions about which bits to do in which order.

It was a sight to behold.

I didn't finish the shirt that weekend. Using my mother-in-law's electric machine I stitched the back to the yoke, then the front, tacked round the neck to stop the fabric pulling, and sewed up the sides and along the arms. Still to do were the cuffs, and the two-part collar, the hem around the bottom of the shirt and the buttonholes.

I hadn't practised, as Lucy recommended, but in the event those bits didn't take long. I was glad to have the chance to finish the job at home in London, on my crazy treadle-powered machine.

When I'd completed those last jobs, I put on the £5 shirt and it fitted beautifully. Nobody had been exploited in the making of it. The finishing, if I say so myself, was superb. I wore it for days on end, washing it in the evening so that it could dry by morning. I had come a long way since standing in my pants in that felt-lined box in Brooks Brothers' Madison Avenue store. But there was more to do. Now, I resolved, I was going to make a complete outfit.

chapter 34

Being Childish

I was finding real value in religion, but still preferred not to join any church formally. At the same time, my experiments with clothes making had reminded me how much I always enjoyed making things, particularly drawings and paintings.

In my own way, I was stumbling towards the realisation that creativity is itself deeply spiritual. And that idea was spelled out for me when I met the artist Billy Childish.

Childish can talk. And talk. At school he was told he had verbal incontinence, and it seems that hasn't changed. He paints, writes, and makes music no less abundantly. He's produced 2,500 pictures, published 40 books of poetry and four novels, and released more than 100 full-length albums – about half as many again as the Rolling Stones, who have been at it twice as long.

"I'm Sagittarius to the power of a million," Childish explains. "And I have that with Jupiter, so I can never do enough – absolutely unlimited pffft!"

Despite his extraordinary output, the chances are that you have not heard of Childish. Or if you have, you only know vaguely that he once went out with Tracey Emin, the artist who has since been showered with acclaim and money.

Childish holds Emin's worldly success in disdain. In 2006, he declined a lucrative offer to appear in Celebrity Big Brother. Indeed, Childish does not watch TV, or listen to the radio, or read newspapers, and hasn't done so for years. He doesn't "do" email or mobile phones, and his web presence is taken care of by somebody else. The last time he went to a gig, other than as performer, was in the 1970s. This helps to explain how he has the time to produce so much work. It also explains his extraordinarily scanty grasp of popular culture. "People think I'm being cute when I don't recognise the names of people they mention," he says.

Nevertheless, Childish has himself been a cult hero to people around the world, including many who are themselves well known and successful. They include the late Kurt Cobain, PJ Harvey, Robert Plant, and Beck. Graham Coxon of Blur once drummed for Childish's band. The White Stripes asked Childish to paint live on stage with them on Top Of The Pops. Kylie Minogue phoned him to ask if she could use the title of one of his poems for one of her albums. ("She was very polite and very nice," he reports.)

His poetry has twice won him National Poetry Prize commendations. The former poet laureate, Andrew Motion, said of Childish: "He looks like he's having more fun being a poet than I am."

As for the art world: Emin has acknowledged his profound influence on her own work, of which more later, and a new critical study of Childish by the artist and writer Neal Brown describes him as "one of the most outstanding, and often misunderstood, figures on the British art scene."

Brown "discovered" Childish in the course of writing a book about Emin for the Tate. He couldn't fathom why nobody was writing similar books about Childish. I can't understand it either.

Childish has been compared with William Blake, and with DH Lawrence – like them, he manages both to write and to paint. But as Brown points out, he also shares their sincerity and eccentric other-worldliness.

When I mentioned these names to Childish, he thought for a moment, then said: "I'm not unique. I come from a tradition which only seems to pop up occasionally." He pauses. "I can imagine how arrogant that will sound, written down." (He's frequently accused of arrogance.) "But what I mean is that I'm just not intimidated. I don't take it too seriously. I'm confident enough to do things regardless of ability. I don't sweat over them. I'm not fussy. It's like cooking: I'm good at that, and I don't need recipes."

As a journalist, I'm accustomed to meeting creative people who know that they're rather special. I've also met a number of crushed souls who, believing themselves to be useless, daren't actually try their hand at anything. Childish is a stunning exception: passionately creative in any discipline, but also substantially indifferent to worldly success.

Having followed him for several months – to an exhibition of his paintings in London, and a combined poetry reading-and-music event – and talked with him both face to face, at his gallery, and several times, at great length, over the phone, I find that Childish has quite some influence on me. I've written poems, produced dozens of sketches and paintings and not a few lino cuts. At his home in Kent I offered him a challenge that I wouldn't dream of suggesting to most serious artists: can we do some painting together?

Childish lives in Chatham, literally around the corner from where Dickens once lived very miserably. The house, owned by Childish's mother, stands on a terrace of bedsits. "Most of the neighbours are alright," says Childish, "but some have issues. You have to listen to them fighting and swearing. The street's sealed off at least once a year."

He shares the house with his wife Julie Winn and his young son (by a previous partner) Huddie. (I briefly glimpse Julie, but she's going out for a sewing class.) It's like something from another time: there seems to be nothing made of plastic. Fixed to the wall in the kitchen is an ancient telephone that still works. There's a wooden desk, a Buddha, colourful flags, innumerable hats of every sort, guitars, and many paintings by Childish. Over the door to the garden, the wall has been decorated with primitive animal images scratched into wet cement.

Childish commissions a lot of work from other people, much of it practical: a hefty ladder leading to the loft, wall panelling, a wooden washboard, and the artwork to go on the cover of his latest album. Some of these things were paid for with art: in return for the ladder, Childish painted a portrait of the carpenter's daughters.

Like the house, Childish himself appears to belong to another era, and not only because of his pointy moustache. Today, he wears a collarless work shirt of the sort worn by Victorian navvies. At other times I've seen him in walking boots with real nails in the sole, and a set of replica 1912 Royal Flying Corps overalls – all items specially made for him by friends.

In recent years, his work has become mellower. He's less likely to be angry than rhapsodic. He acknowledges the influence of Jesus Christ and the Buddha.

"We're all stardust," he might say these days. "Nothing new is coming into being. Everything just changes shape and form. My nose, for example, was once a Tyrannosaurus's toe nail."

Or: "You have to take life very seriously, and realise that it's all a joke. That is the art of living."

An equally important aspects of living is making art. "The question of what is art is "very, very simple", he says. "Would the person do it if he wasn't being paid? This would eradicate all of contemporary art! You don't pickle sharks in your shed for 20 years because you believe in it.

"The good thing about art is that no matter how bad it is, if it's lying in the street people will recognise it as art. Whereas a lot of the work we have these days would not be."

People should do more art, he believes. "George Orwell, working as a policeman in Burma, had to practice drawing because they didn't have cameras. This happened a lot in the services. My grandfather was a carpenter in the navy and he had to be able to draw. And the officers too. You had to be able to record things, to convey ideas. And that enables you to see, rather than just look. If you draw something then you can actually see it. And you will see things in the world around you. Drawing and painting open up the natural world. Painting is the medium of self-discovery.

"When I was a kid, from three to six, my painting was loose. Then it was colourful from 11 to 16, then dark and graphic as a 21- to 33-year-old drunk. Since 33, I've just been working backwards again. That's when I became an adult, at 33, and gave up drink and inverted anger."

Other people don't produce half as much work as him. Why is that? "I have to pretend I don't do as much as I do, because it embarrasses me. People sometimes ask me and I pretend I haven't done anything recently."

He's prolific, it seems, not only because he doesn't watch telly or read the papers but because he's fast. "I paint a picture in 15 minutes, maybe 20, sometime three-quarters of an hour; if it's all going to hell, 3 hours. Sometimes time and effort rescues it, but usually it just tortures it. Most times I like the first go, then come back a couple of hours later and decide whether to add one tiny brush mark; that's the touch that pleases my soul."

He's sometimes asked to teach in art schools. As a result, he says, the students produce more in one afternoon than in the rest of the term. "I try to get them to let go, and use no skill whatever. This is an absolute block. They're so tied up because they can't bring themselves to do rubbish."

But why should they? Isn't the point of being students that they want to move beyond producing rubbish?

"When people say their kids could do such and such a painting, my smart answer is, "Well I would expect your kids to do it, but can you? It takes a lot of work to get that free and easy – to be natural. Skilful means effortless. You can get that with beginners luck but after that you have to do some more work to recapture it, which is what Picasso talked about. It takes a lot of effort to get back to effortlessness, not to draw like an uptight artist.

"I've been working between the tension of my skill and allowing the painting to be as it wants to be since I was 33. The first trick was to not care what others might think of my work. The next was to paint and not care what I thought about it myself. Basically, I don't bother impressing others, then step it up a gear and don't bother impressing myself. That is where you get real freedom. That is the big one. That's why I work quickly, and why I don't look at it again for another week. (He paints on Sundays, at his mother's house.) "So I can see it as if it was done by someone else."

This does not mean that he considers all his raw work to be brilliant. But he seems relaxed about work that turns out badly. "I saw some of my paintings today and I'm appalled by them." For most artists to say that would be devastating, but to Childish it's just five minutes' annoyance.

The interesting thing about painting pictures, he concludes, is painting pictures. And with music, the interesting thing is playing it. "When I was a child, people got together and played in the pub, and in the car park. And people knew how to do a turn. They were not having to make do with what was dumped on them.

"People think I'm an amateur. That's become a derogatory term, like I don't know what I'm doing. But the amateur is someone who does things out of love."

In keeping with the amateurism is his cussedly uncommercial approach. At his gallery, his dealer Steve Lowe showed me copies of the latest Childish novel, The Idiocy of Idears. It was the second edition, Lowe explained, the first having been printed with no price on the cover – indeed, with a notice saying that shoppers should refuse to pay anything at all for it. Copies had been distributed around bookshops all over London. Similarly, after being told that he was committing commercial suicide by releasing too much music, one of his bands, Thee Milkshakes (*sic*), released four LPs in a single day.

Plainly, he doesn't care about money: "If you want to be rich," he tells me at one point, "value what you have got."

I ask him why he has given me so much of his time over the last few months.

He gives it a moment's thought. "I like to influence people."

He takes me into the office and sits in front of Julie's gleaming Apple computer – the first piece of plastic high-tech I've seen in the house. He opens various music files: tracks from his latest album, Thatcher's Children. He plays them to me, and every so often laughs unashamedly at the lyrics. It turns out that several of the songs were written by Julie, and sung by her too.

"Most of my girlfriends have ended up painting or singing," he says. And if there's one thing that hanging around with Childish has taught me, it's this: "Creativity is our birthright. But the English don't like people who are self-taught. They haven't passed the driving test. It's not about whether you can do it, but did you go through the right channels?"

This is an incredibly empowering idea, and all the more worthwhile because – to put this bluntly – not absolutely everything Childish does seems to me to be all that wonderfully brilliant. I hugely admire the energy of his music, for instance, and share his amusement at many of the lyrics, but on balance it's sometimes a bit of a racket.

Still, listening to the music has cheered him up immensely. I remind him that he's promised to do some painting with me but we're running out of time. A friend of his – a member of the Band of Historical Hillwalkers – is coming round soon to dress up in tweed, wool and leather (Velcro and Gore-Tex are discouraged) then set out to breathe the air (as the Hillwalkers Manifesto, written by Childish, puts it) and engage with the world by making pinhole photographs and painting.

Childish whizzes me back into the kitchen. Looking through my sketchbooks very rapidly he says my drawings look a bit "tight", but stops to commend one rather hasty study of pine cones.

We tear pages from the huge sketchbook I brought, and throw tubes of paint all over the floor – and in the next 15 minutes we produce no fewer than eight paintings of each other. By the time his hillwalking friend has arrived, the entire kitchen floor is covered in paintings.

The colours are in no way realistic, and the shapes aren't always right either. "Is my head really that heart-shaped," he asks at one point. Another time, he laughs at one of my pictures and says, correctly, that it looks a bit boss eyed. I can't say that I'm pleased. Painting at speed was exhilarating, but I leave the paintings with him to dry and for weeks make no effort to retrieve them. They're worthless – and I don't only mean in monetary terms.

Some days later, Childish sends me an email – itself rather a surprise. I almost junk it because he uses one of his many pseudonyms – in this case, William Claudius. The email consists of a poem he wrote the previous night, inspired by our recent conversation: "some say im/ laurence/some say im/ blake/ some say im/ true/ some say im/ fake," it starts.

I phone him to say thanks, and while he's on the line I ask why he wanted me to paint so fast. He's talked and written often enough about the need for sincerity and authenticity in art – couldn't I have achieved those at a slightly slower pace? Or was it simply that we'd run out of time?

Not at all, he insists. We worked fast, he goes on to explain, to feel truly alive: "Every artist knows that if they get something in a sketch it can be impossible to recapture that energy in another medium. And that's the kind of energy I'm trying to get into everything. When you paint, you're in the moment.

"Creativity is the only thing that engages with life. It's the joining of mind and material. It's a spiritual thing – and all of life should be like that."

chapter 35

*In which the author attempts to re-establish
the Victorian Workhouse*

I'd learned a lot about how creative work could be spiritually uplifting, and also economically sensible.

Some months after I joined the board of the neighbouring elderly care home, it dawned on me to try getting a spot of creative work into the lives of the sometimes rather bored-looking residents.

If Fry could improve things for prisoners by giving them materials and tools, and Gandhi could do the same for Indians, perhaps I could help the aged? After all, I'd seen how Great-Aunt Peggy was gripped by the task of helping me to make my shirt.

But could I really get the residents knitting? I went to see the manager, and the woman who valiantly strives to entertain them, and then asked the residents themselves. Quite a few looked positively delighted by the idea.

At first, I thought they might do the odd scarf for me, but gradually realised that it would be better to make a genuine business out of it. I remembered reading that during the Great Irish Famine of the 1840s Ursuline nuns taught local women and children to crochet. Their work was shipped all across Europe and America and purchased for its beauty and also for the charitable help it provided for the Irish population.

I went online to look for a load of knitting needles and crochet hooks. I didn't find any, but got sidetracked by an extraordinarily interesting blog by a woman in Colorado, showing how to take apart charity-shop sweaters and unravel the wool for re-use. I wondered if I could get some of the old ladies to do that, too? Perhaps Traid could let me have the jumpers? I sent Lyla Patel an email, begging very politely, and another one congratulating the woman in Colorado.

Getting just a little carried away, I wondered whether I might sign up residents at other care homes, too? Put together a whole army of elderly clothes makers? They could form a cooperative and sell their stuff online through a craft community such as Etsy.com. Or perhaps I could get them work for People Tree, the ethical clothing company that usually relies on knitters in Bangladesh, and other places far from home?

In effect, I had all-but reinvented (though only in my imagination) the Victorian Workhouse. And why not? After all, work is nourishing and enlivening, according to Schumacher. Conducted in conditions of human dignity and freedom, it blesses those who do it and equally their products.

Come to that, children should have work too. I had failed, so far, to interest Nancy in crochet and knitting but hoped to remedy that by getting residents in the care home to teach her.

What about her cousins? My sister-in-law Julia, who lives just round the corner from us, has three sons. Not altogether surprisingly, none of the boys – Joe, Reuben and the youngest, Zac, who had long ago decorated my washable suit with ice cream – had shown any sign of being interested in knitting or crochet, but their mother, who now works in senior management in the health service, did study textiles at school and once even kept a sizeable loom in the sitting room of her London flat (to the great dismay of Harriet, who shared the flat).

On a visit to Julia and the boys, one Sunday afternoon when they were mostly doing homework and thus willing to show an interest in virtually anything else, I demonstrated a simple and quick way to cut a plastic carrier bag into a single ribbon of "plarn" (plastic yarn). I'd seen how to do this on the internet, and was frankly delighted to find a new way to use carrier bags that I didn't need, and had recently used purposefully only once, as a shroud for rats.

Then, while we drank tea and ate cakes, I used a 4.5mm crochet hook to turn the yarn into a tiny little basket, with a lid that could be fixed shut. As I worked, I thought with great joy that I was saving the bag from the fate of millions of others like it, reviled items used only once before being dumped in landfill such as the site I'd seen as a dustman.

Julia pronounced herself impressed, as did her husband David and all three boys. Julia told the oldest he should take the basket to school and show it to his teacher. He agreed that this might be a good idea, but didn't seem quite so keen on her subsequent suggestion that his uncle should come and teach everybody in his class to crochet.

Still, it was a start.

Next, I went to see Camila Batmanghelidjh, whom I've known for several years since I first wrote about her extraordinary work with literally thousands of disturbed and often violent children living in south London. Many of these children are brought up, effectively, by their siblings or their peers, because their parents are all too often dead, addicted to mind-altering substances, or in jail. Quite a number never attend school and don't even exist, so far as officialdom is concerned. Many turn up at the premises of Camila's charity, Kids Company, determined to cause trouble – because that's the only mode they've learned.

It was lovely to see Camila again. She told me how some of the children I had met were now getting on. One small group of former child-soldiers, previously hardened to rape and cold-blooded slaughter, had recently been enrolled at higher education establishments and took Camila out to celebrate over a pizza.

I told Camila that I had a plan to help her in bringing a sense of useful purpose into the children's lives. It was this: she should get somebody (me, if necessary) to teach them crochet. They'd love it. I could show them how to make "plarn" (plastic yarn) out of carrier bags, and they would never lack for raw materials. Who knows, perhaps they could sell what they made?

"We need to stop kids carrying knives," I announced, "and get them to carry crochet hooks instead."

Camila didn't absolutely leap into the air, but she smiled and agreed that it was a nice idea.

And there's nothing wrong with spreading ideas. Soon after, Camila sent me an email.

"I'm going to bear in mind your gift in knitting. I wonder whether we should start a knitting marathon and fundraise for it."

I replied: "I think a knitting marathon is a great idea. But don't forget crochet – the hooks (not as sharp as they sound!) are more portable than a pair of much longer knitting needles. I have visions of young people crocheting hoodies on street corners."

And the next time I visited Julia, my sister-in-law, she surprised me by handing over an old school textbook on weaving, and saying she was thinking about buying a new loom, and her own spinning wheel.

Result!

chapter 36

*While his wife is out, the author makes a pair
of jeans. For the fly, he uses spare buttons
from old cheap suits, including the washable
one from M&S*

My outfit was coming along nicely. I had made a shirt, darned socks, and taken apart a pair of boxer shorts to fit new elastic in the waistband. I was still knitting a jumper. A pair of jeans would complete the outfit. I wanted very much to be able to stand fully clothed and say that every item had been either made or modified by me.

Meanwhile, I'd struck out into Hinduism, reading passages of the *Baghavad Gita* that I knew meant a great deal to Gandhi. One in particular stressed the importance of doing whatever you do with no attachment whatever to the outcome.

For a week or so, very much aware of these teachings from the East, I suppressed my jeans-making yearning. But then one night before closing time I snuck out to Desai, the local fabric shop, while Harriet watched TV with Nancy, and came home with 2.5m of very heavy denim indeed – the only kind Desai had in stock.

I wasn't absolutely in love with the fabric, much stiffer than the jeans I normally wear and also very dark indigo, while I tend to favour the faded look.

But I had been wearing faded, darned jeans for too long. And I was damned if I was going to spend £150 or more on a new pair from one of the fancy shops that stocks the very nice jeans I'd become accustomed to wearing.

So I popped the heavy denim into the washing machine and selected a fairly hot wash – to shrink the material before I made the jeans. And with heavy heart I started to unpick my favourite jeans.

The unpicker broke.

So I went to Chinsardy, the dressmakers round the corner, where Lucy lent me a heavy duty unpicker. Thus armed, I snipped through the jeans in no time, though I was unable to smash the metal studs, even using a heavy mallet. (I cut round them.) Then I went back to Chinsardy to ask if I could have some of the heavy brown paper Lucy uses to make patterns. She very kindly gave me a few yards for nothing, saying I could pay her back with a present at Christmas. (I did: a selection of biscuits custom-made by a friend, Pru, to look like dresses and scissors and clothes patterns.)

I should stress that, just like the bookcase, I did this while Harriet was at work. But when she came home, it didn't take her long to notice the too-dark jeans. "What are you wearing?" she demanded.

I told her, and twirled a couple of times. She wasn't sure about the colour, but had to admit I'd got the cut right, and the seams too. She could hardly believe how well I'd done the pockets.

But when I sat down the effect was spoiled. The cardboard-stiffness of the denim made the ankles hold their shape around my ankle instead of flopping softly.

This was no good: Harriet said I was not to wear the jeans outside, except just possibly on the allotment where, as part of my strategy to prepare for climate change and peak oil, I was growing my own food.

I was disappointed, but on reflection welcomed the setback because it gave me a chance to practice the detachment that I'd learned from Billy Childish and the *Baghavad Gita*.

chapter 37

How German soldiers, during World War One, went into battle wearing nettle, and why we might all soon to do the same (wear nettle, that is, not go into battle)

In my garden, hacking back a too-vigorous jasmine myself, rather than pay a gardener to come in and do the work for a big fee, and thereby disempower me, I decided for fun to weave a basket out of the cuttings.

As I did so, I suddenly realised what I must always have known, but taken for granted – that many of our finest fabrics come from weaving plant material. And not only plants, but also fibres from animals that share with plants a dependence on the land.

And it occurred to me that, just as we in London have insufficient space to grow our own food, we also lack space to grow fibres for clothing.

With productive land being set aside to grow agrofuels, and riots over food scarcity in several countries, a surprising number of people have come to understand the need to source food locally. (The waiting list for allotments has shot up.) But what about local clothes? Few people have the slightest idea, I suspect, that crop failures associated with climate change, and fuel shortages, will soon lead us back to making clothes out of local materials.

Will we be able to do that?

The question was brought home to me one afternoon when Nancy helped to unpack our weekly delivery of local, seasonal fruit and vegetables. As if reading my mind, she peeled a couple of leaves off a cabbage and fashioned for herself a pair of shoes. The basic idea was sound, but cabbage leaves are unlikely to hold up with heavy use.

To find out who was doing anything more practical about local clothing, I turned to the Transition Town movement that has done so much to promote the idea of self-reliance in food.

"Local food is relatively easy to obtain," I was told by Rose Liles, of Transition Town Stroud. "But local clothes and other fibres are not. What we'd really like to do in Stroud is to get fabric production going again in this area. This town has a long and proud heritage in making textiles."

But that heritage is largely forgotten. A paradoxical effect of being a colonial power is that people in Britain, having relied for so long on cheap cotton from overseas, have forgotten which local materials can be used for textiles: in our own way, we're victims of colonial history too.

Liles and her friends in Stroud's textiles group have worked hard to raise awareness of these issues. Among other things, they've taught knitting and sewing skills and encouraged people to buy from second-hand stalls in farmers markets and online.

They've also tried to grow one of the ancient British textile crops, hemp, to make cloth. Working with Stroudwater Textile Trust and other local producers, they plan to establish a "Stroud Hemporium", a co-operative to manufacture clothes from home-grown domestic textiles, as well as refurbishing machinery at local mills.

This has not worked out entirely successfully: "The first crop was eaten by deer," Liles reports.

I must confess that when I first heard about hemp for clothing I thought immediately that this was bound to be second-rate, suitable only for shabby dope-fiends and beardy-weirdies. I was mistaken. Check out this fulsome plaudit, which I found online, from an American clothes-maker:

"Of all the fabrics that I have known and loved, my favourite is Romanian hemp. Hemp fabrics from Romania are as rich and textured as the history of hemp itself. When I opened my first packet of Romanian hemp fabric swatches I felt a tingling sensation like I was discovering an ancient treasure.

"Any well designed and well executed product made from these materials has a feeling of heirloom to it. And in this day and age when most of our belongings are designed out of materials and made in such a way as to last only a season or two, or maybe a few years at the most, this trait of longevity is truly a gift.

"What more beautiful plant is there than this hempen plant for naturally treading lightly on the planet?"

Quite so. Hemp is resistant to pests so requires no chemical pesticides or fungicides. It's fast-growing, so it chokes out weeds and requires no herbicides. The long fibres are broken free from the stalk with nothing but water, before being spun into yarn and woven into fabric.

Come to think of it, Darryl Hannah had made some rather amazing claims for hemp: she told me it could be turned into any manufactured product that isn't made of glass or metal. And having seen for myself how much work Hannah puts into her investigations I had no reason to disbelieve her.

Why isn't hemp more widely used? Under Henry VIII, hemp was considered so useful that it was illegal *not* to grow a bit of it. Now we've gone the other way, because the plant is related to cannabis and, though entirely free of narcotic effect, it cannot be grown legally except with a Home Office licence, and even then only if it's locked away from public access.

Well, I don't have a licence, but I do have a garden that's inaccessible to passers by. So last summer I illegally sowed a handful of hemp seeds I'd bought in a health-food shop. It was late in the year, and the seeds had little time to grow and I had only a few very short plants by the autumn. I cut them, and left them on the ground to "ret" (the Dutch word for rot, favoured for some mysterious reason by the textile trade). After that, I peeled a few strands of hair-thin bark and twisted them into a short but incredibly strong piece of thread – hurrah! It sat on my desk for several weeks, a much prized trophy, until it was swept away by persons unknown and presumably put out with the rubbish.

But there's another native plant we might use in future: the nettle.

Ray Harwood, formerly of de Montfort University's Nettle Project, told me all about it. In the early years of the 20th century, he explained, Britain controlled 90 per cent of world cotton. And for reasons that must be obvious, Austro-Hungary and Germany were keen to develop alternatives – acutely so, by the time of the First World War, in which they would have had to fight naked if cotton became unavailable.

The work of developing an alternative was overseen by a man legendary in the admittedly small nettle-fibre industry: Professor G Bredeman of Hamburg University spent decades trying to grow the finest varieties of nettle, and continued doing so into the Second World War and beyond.

By then, the British cotton industry had been all-but destroyed, what with Gandhi teaching Indians to weave themselves and American cotton supplies cut off by the U-boats. But, alas, the nettle's big moment was ruined by the advent of cheap synthetics, not just in Britain but everywhere, even including Germany.

Bredeman's research was not altogether in vain, however, because in 1990 it was rediscovered by members of the University of Hamburg Institute of Applied Botany. They found live nettles, and photographs, and samples of nettle fabric. Nine years later, with EU backing, companies in Germany, Austria and Italy started to look into developing nettles commercially, using clones of high-fibre nettles cultivated over many years by Bredeman.

Unlike hemp, the nettle is a perennial, which means that it can be propagated vegetatively. After six weeks in the greenhouse, cuttings are transplanted to the field. There is no crop in the first year as the plants need to establish themselves but afterwards the plants can be harvested year after year. The yield in the second year is between 1.5 and 2.5 metric tonnes per hectare. By the third and fourth year the harvest could amount to 4 tonnes, or 4,000 kilos. It takes about 40 kilos to provide enough material for one shirt, so a hectare of nettles could in its third year of production provide fibre for 100 shirts – as well as a great quantity of by-products, including sugar, starch, protein and ethyl alcohol, not forgetting leaves to eat as a vegetable or use as a tea.

At night, after watching particularly gloomy stories on the evening news about climate change or failing energy supplies, I cheer myself up by imagining that the future won't be all bad if we can only get our act together and start cultivating more nettles, and hemp.

Why not let's do this Gandhi style, by encouraging just about everybody to grown just a small amount, for collection, spinning and weaving locally? Me, I could grow some nettle (and just possibly hemp, if I got a licence) on my allotment.

But when I contacted Britain's only major processor, Hemcore, with this idea I was told: "We are not able to produce textiles from growing hemp here in the UK. It needs a further non mechanical step after decortications. We are researching this but we have not solved the problem so far. If you grew hemp on your allotment you would not be able to produce textile grade hemp I'm afraid."

I found this hard to understand. How did people manage in the middle ages?

Maybe Hemcore is just too big. Perhaps this really does need to be a cottage industry. I would have to process the plants, then spin and weave the fibres myself.

A year after talking to Liles about her experiments with hemp, I called another member of Transition Stroud's textile group, Emily Smith. She told me they had recently held a workshop on nettle fibre. Somebody brought in some long-stemmed nettles, and everybody set about trying to extract fibre. By her account, the whole thing was rather fun.

"The ones that were most successful had the thickest, woody stems," Smith said. "We just bashed them. Every so often up the stem you find a ring, where the leaves were, and then bash those rings and split it lengthways with a knife and open it out and pull out the hard inside. Then peel off the fibres in bundles and then pull them apart. You can get quite long fibres. We twisted them together and they formed a cord. We twisted various lengths, from very fine – less than 1mm thick, for sewing – to very thick. It was really strong. Even the individual fibres we couldn't break."

Nettle fabric, experts report, is good quality because the fibres can be long: anything above $1^3/_8$ inch is equal to the best Egyptian cotton. Nettle can be dyed and bleached in the same way as cotton, and when mercerized is only slightly inferior to silk. It has been considered much superior to cotton for velvet and plush. In fact nettle fabric can be such good stuff that, as a publicity stunt,

Harwood and his colleagues had a load of nettle turned into a bikini. You can still see the pictures on the internet.

Inspired by this unusual outfit, I decided to use my power as a consumer to encourage material manufacturers to use nettle. I found what appears to be the only material made in Britain with nettle as a component: a sturdy nettle-wool blend from Camira Fabrics in Yorkshire. It was designed for use in furniture, but I remembered Vivienne Westwood urging people to make clothes out of curtains, and decided that this didn't matter.

I bought enough to make a waistcoat.

Next, I tried to find a website selling unprocessed nettle fibre. I could find nothing in Britain, but there was somebody in northern France, which is local enough, for now.

I bought a load, then got in touch with Brenda Gibson of the London Guild of Spinners and Weavers, who kindly agreed to help me to spin it herself.

chapter 38

Welcome to the world of shoemaking

After a year of use, my (literally) green sneakers were finally coming to the end of their (very) natural lives.

They'd had a tough workout, but the various sustainable materials, including hemp and jute and natural latex, coped well. The laces went first, but I darned the bits together (yes, I know!) and carried on as if nothing had happened. But now the soles had gone, and I concluded that it must all be over.

Then I thought – No!

After all, the manufacturer is the admirable Simple shoes, which I first came across as sponsor of the Chronicles of Dan Price, a latter day Thoreau (whose delightful work I recommend very strongly). What's more, I recently had a pair of Timberlands resoled, despite considerable reluctance on the part of my local cobbler (he said they had to be sent back to the manufacturer, but the manufacturer proved by no means keen, so I took them back to him and he improvised with great success).

If Timberlands can be saved, why not Simples? Perhaps I could get my Men's Toemorrow (as the sneakers are called) resoled too? After all, the uppers are OK, and if I keep them going rather than buy a new pair, that's got to be good for the planet etc.

But was it even possible to get this done? Did I have to send the shoes to the US? Or could Simple send me new soles, for somebody in London – me, for instance – to glue in place?

I found Simple's website and phoned somebody in California who proved very friendly. There was a bit of a misunderstanding, at first, because she thought that I only wanted a new inner sole ("No problem!") and when I explained that I wanted a new piece of rubber to go underneath the shoe, she reported with regret that this was not possible.

But she saved the day by pointing out that Simple makes a do-it-yourself shoe kit. For just $15, I could buy an oddly shaped piece of leather with rubber soles and tough thread with which to sew it together.

Naturally, I bought the kit, which came with step-by-step instructions.

"Hello and welcome to the world of shoemaking," it read. "We know that you like to make all kinds of stuff – arts, crafts, a mess. Whatever. Well, you're just an afternoon away from adding shoes to your list of accomplishments. Take your time. Enjoy your first day as a shoemaker, cuz wearing shoes is fine and dandy but the real fun is in the making."

I couldn't agree more, though I was sad to see that Simple found it necessary to add a disclaimer of warranty, stating that it would in no event be liable to me or any other person for any special or punitive damages, of any kind or nature, arising out of the completion or use of this product by me or any other person and any related injuries of any kind or nature.

I sewed the shoes together, without experiencing injury or other hardship of any kind or nature. It was a fairly simple process – stitching up either side of the heel, then around the tongue. I confess that the resulting shoe does not absolutely look like something from Manolo Blahnik – but that didn't matter, because I could now report, correctly, that I had made my own shoes.

chapter 39

Prick your finger

A few weeks later, after the nettle fibre arrived, I went to Gibson's home in south London. I didn't know what to expect, but was intrigued, because on the phone she had gone out of her way to stress that she, like her colleagues in the guild, was "not beardy weirdy".

She did indeed look entirely normal, in white blouse and pale trousers and a navy cardigan that I doubted she had had anything to do with making.

Over coffee, she told me she first got involved in the fibre arts after her husband asked what she might like as a present for her birthday. She had been reading something about spinning wheels, and casually suggested he buy her one.

In the years since then, working as a regulator in the City, she had found the repetitive, tactile action of spinning extremely therapeutic; indeed, sometimes she would spin throughout the weekend, to unwind (as it were).

With time she expanded her interests, so that today she has a whole den, on the second-floor, filled with spinning equipment, a number of looms, balls and skeins of every kind of yarn, and extraordinarily beautiful fabric samples, including one that, as if by magic, retained a solid, staircase-like ridge down the middle while remaining flat on the outside.

In the den, Gibson showed me a charka – the horizontal spinning wheel Gandhi used, with a double-wheel drive making it portable (for people who like to spin at political meetings). But while the charka is great for spinning cotton, it would not be so suitable for spinning nettle.

So she went away and brought back a hefty rucksack containing a portable spinning wheel of more familiar western design.

She took a small handful of the nettle fibre I'd brought and teased it out a little, then attached it to a thread already fixed to the bobbin and – after connecting a few bits together – she began to work the treadle gently, which spun the wheel, which in turn put a twist into the fibre, turning what had previously been diffuse into a tight, strong yarn. Releasing this carefully, she allowed it to be pulled onto the bobbin as she fed more of the fluffy "wool" onto the end to be twisted in its turn.

It was my turn now. At first, I felt like I was doing rather well. In fact, Gibson called me a "natural", which was gratifying, but since virtually everybody used to be able to spin till relatively recently, I could hardly regard this as a great compliment. Anyway, the thing that impressed her was how easily I took to the treadle – and since I have something similar on my sewing machine, I wasn't exactly a novice.

I wanted to know how much yarn I might eventually spin out of the 100g of fibre I had bought.

Gibson took out a weighing device and cut a length of the yarn she'd already spun. After snipping away at the end for a while, the device went into balance. So she measured the yarn on a yardstick on her table, did a quick calculation, and announced that I would eventually have more than 700m.

I was impressed. How long would it take me to spin the lot?

It varies, she said. Not only because I am not practiced but also because different yarns, spun to different thicknesses, require different amounts of work.

She took out a single skein of white bamboo fibre she'd recently spun herself. Spinning this, she said, took her eight hours.

Eight hours! At the time of writing, the national minimum wage is £5.52 an hour. So a single ball of bamboo yarn, if you paid somebody to spin it, would cost at least £45, and that's assuming that the fibre cost nothing. To make a man's sweater you'd need several skeins, and if you wanted somebody to knit that for you, you'd pay for a similar amount of time. We're talking about something like £500 for a sweater.

It's true that we don't need to pay that much, because we have machines to do the work for us. But as we've seen, the fuel required to propel those machines, and to ship the raw materials and finished goods back and forth around the globe, is liable to run out in the not-too distant future. We could carry on as we are till the oil runs out, but if we want to save oil for other useful purposes, and limit global warming, we'd better stop doing that. In which case, welcome to the world of the £500 sweater.

Or, more optimistically, welcome to the world in which everybody can enjoy once again the processes involved in making their own clothes.

And this really could be good news, and not only because the processes can be therapeutic. Additionally, Gibson believes, the finished goods can be of much higher quality than most people wear today: this was certainly the case in the Middle Ages, and fabrics found inside Egyptian tombs show evidence of extremely fine work, she added, even though they must have been spun on homely machines.

After I'd spun some more nettle, I said I might quite like to get a spinning wheel at home, and asked how much it cost. Maybe about £300, she suggested.

Hm. I didn't know what Harriet would think: it had been hard enough for her to accept the sewing machine. But surely she'd see the benefits if I spun while we watched telly? Did Gibson do that?

Yes, she said. But it annoyed her husband, who had to turn up the volume.

She suggested I might save quite a bit of money and eliminate the noise problem, by spinning with a drop-spindle instead.

To show how this works, she took one from a shelf. It looked like a knitting needle shoved through a very thick wooden dish. Again, she tied a bit of the nettle wool to a thread already attached, dropped the spindle, spinning, into the air in front of her knees and let the yarn twist.

"It's cheaper, but less efficient – and you get tired arms," she concluded.

I asked her about wool. Ken, the farmer who lives next-door to my in-laws in Somerset told me once that nobody wants the wool from his sheep. He literally can't give it away, and shearing costs him a small fortune. This didn't seem right.

Gibson pointed to a basket in a corner of the room containing dozens of balls of wool she'd spun from a single fleece. It was coarse, but after dying it came up nicely and would do well for a rug, or a wall-hanging, she said.

Before leaving, I asked Gibson why she had made such a point, on the telephone, of telling me she wasn't beardy-weirdy.

"Because people seem to expect that," she said. "A TV company wanted to film us spinning recently, and asked if we would dress in 'period' costume. 'Which period do you want?' we asked."

I liked Gibson, and felt inspired by what she had shown me. I wondered whether I could persuade my sister-in-law to buy a loom as she'd discussed. Or perhaps I could get one, and a spinning wheel too, for residents to use in the care home?

Hoping to find out more, I crossed London to pop into the boutique Prick Your Finger, where you can buy pretty well any local and ethical yarn you care to mention. The owners, Rachael Matthews and Louise Harries, had just finished spinning some in the back room when I arrived.

They gave me a brisk tour of the various yarns and explained the quite extraordinary variety: one kind of sheep produces wool with a shine, said Matthews. Another is incredibly coarse, but if you made an outer garment it would be virtually waterproof. Then there are British alpacas, and angora from rabbits…

I told Matthews about Ken, the farmer in Somerset, and his problem sheep. Many fleeces go unused, she said, because nobody wants the coarse stuff: even insulating your attic with it, or laying it under carpets, requires a certain amount of expensive processing.

The shop is full of funny things Matthews and Harries have knitted and crocheted themselves, as documented in the cheerfully inspiring books Knitorama and Hookerama – knitted cutlery, crocheted cup and saucer. The shop sign at the front comprises knitted woollen letters, reading Prick Your Finger, 18 inches high.

One item that particularly amused me was made by their friend Lauren Porter – a full-sized crocheted bathroom suite. But when I later showed a picture of the bathroom suite to Harriet, she asked if it wasn't a bit of a waste of good material.

I was stumped – but only for a second. Did anybody say that about all the steel that went into Antony Gormley's Angel of the North? Or the stone used by Michelangelo?

chapter 40

Apprenticed in Savile Row

I was happy to agree, with Brenda Gibson, that people who spin, weave and make clothes are not beardy weirdy, and that the clothes they wear are first-rate. But I fear that many people won't see it that way. They'll think that home-made clothes, made with materials that are "good for the planet", must be ghastly. How could I show that's not true?

An answer suggested itself when *The Sunday Times* asked me to write about the British government's recent drive to promote old-fashioned apprenticeships. I agreed, and lined up a stint – for one day only – as an apprentice at the esteemed Savile Row tailors Anderson & Sheppard. This might help, albeit in the tiniest way, to close the British "skills gap".

Since the economic collapse of the 1980s, many once-thriving industries have offloaded the work overseas. As a result, few young people in Britain have skills that were once taken for granted – including, as we've seen, the ability to make clothes. Tailoring, as carried out at Anderson & Sheppard, is a special case and survives only because it's so specialised. Most of the rest of the rag trade has vanished.

I was apprenticed to the managing director, John Hitchcock. I watched him closely as he made a pair of trousers for me in the morning ("you'll enjoy wearing these," he predicted correctly) and in the afternoon I made a similar pair for him.

On such experiences is a great apprenticeship based. After all, Mr Hitchcock is Prince Charles's personal tailor. As a young tailor, he learned from Mr Bryant, and Mr Bryant learned from the firm's founder, Mr Anderson.

While I was with him, I also met a pair of students on day release from Newham College, hand stitching many hundreds of the 20,000 hand-stitches that go into each jacket.

"Nice work!" Mr Hitchcock told them. But afterwards, out of earshot, he revealed that the students will be given the collars they're working on to take home and show their parents. "It would be unkind to put them in the bin in front of them."

Many UK-based skilled manual jobs have been filled in recent years by migrants, such as a million or so Poles and other "new" Europeans. Now a lot of them are returning home, thanks to the collapsing pound. Can Britons fill the gap? Not necessarily, because rather than encourage people into vocational learning, the government has spent a decade promoting university education – promising that graduates can expect to earn zillions as a result of having a degree.

Which turns out – big surprise – to be an exaggeration. Over the past decade, British students have amassed an astonishing £27bn mountain of debt – as much as £37,000 each. Many, after a decade in work, aren't yet earning £15,000 a year – the threshold at which they start to pay back student loans. As one recent graduate complains on an internet discussion board: "If I could go back to when I was a teen, I would almost definitely do a trade of some description. I have a degree now but one of my biggest regrets is never doing a trade."

Leaving graduates aside, Britain boasts more 16- to 18-year-olds out of work – or not receiving education – than almost any developed nation: we come 24th of 28 countries. And jobless teenagers cost Britain £250m a year, according to the CBI.

In short: we've exported skilled jobs overseas, hired migrants to do what's needed here, pushed disproportionate numbers of young people into academic higher education, and kept many others unqualified and expensively unemployable.

From the employer's point of view, the case for apprenticeships is compelling. Three-quarters say apprentices improve their company's productivity; a third even maintain that they do so within their first weeks. Sixty per cent agree that training apprentices is cheaper than hiring skilled staff – though this doesn't entirely re-assure Anderson & Sheppard, whose co-chairman Anda Rowland worries that, once qualified, her apprentices may be snapped up by other tailors who don't put themselves to the trouble of providing training.

Rowland has identified a major shift in attitudes among young people, away from the stereotypical media-studies degree towards learning proper trades. Mr Hitchcock concurs: "For a while, no one was interested. But this is like organic food: people want to go back to how things used to be done."

After lunch, in Anderson & Sheppard's roomy dressing room, I measured up Mr Hitchcock for his trousers.

"Steady on!" he said, as I took his inside leg just a little too forcefully, a lump in his throat, his eyes watering. "Usually, we're a little gentler with our customers."

Setting aside the unfortunate incident with the measuring tape, the day went well. Mr Hitchcock, as we apprentices are honoured to call him, watched closely as I cut, pressed and sewed, so little could go wrong; but all the same I was pleased that he considered my finished work satisfactory. Indeed, he promised to wear the trousers I had made him.

chapter 41

Forbidden to wear his homemade jeans publicly, the author meets the unusual Guy Hills, who cheerfully cycles round London in luminous plus-fours and cape

---

What with all the training I'd had, I was starting to wonder if I was right to let Harriet determine what I wear outside the house.

My doubts were compounded after I met a man who cycles cheerfully round London in plus fours and cape – in a fabric striped with luminous fibres to ensure that he shows up at night.

As it happens, Guy Hills was at university with me, though we didn't really know each other then. But it was impossible not to notice him, wearing the outfit just described, outside the gates of Nancy's school. It turned out that his own young son attends the same place.

If this already seems like an unlikely coincidence, you will probably not care to believe that I had been talking about Hills only days earlier, during my apprenticeship at Anderson & Sheppard. Mr Hitchcock had mentioned that some of the younger tailors were working with a chap who created luminous tweeds, and happened to name Hills.

The last I'd heard about him was some years ago, from a mutual friend who worked on a fashion magazine. At the time, Hills was working as a photographer. This turned out to be how he got to know the tailors on Savile Row – by photographing them at work. His pictures were used in their publicity, and in exchange, Hills was paid not in cash but with a number of items of fitted clothing.

I marched up to him at the school gate and told him my name. He claimed to remember me from university, and confirmed what I'd been told.

He gave me a card, bearing the name of his business, Dashing Tweeds. He said he had set up a weaver in a studio nearby, where she designed tweeds that were then woven in bulk in Harris.

I was impressed by his bouncy enthusiasm, and gladly accepted an invitation to pop over to his house and look at some of his tweeds, and his tailored outfits.

Over leftover, home-made children's birthday cake, Hills told me he had always appreciated things that were well made, and became interested in tailored clothing after finding his wife (then still his girlfriend) being chatted up by a well-dressed soldier. He went to intervene, and ended up being put in touch with an army tailor.

That was eight years ago. Hills contacted the tailor, got himself a suit in grey flannel and loved it, but found that, as a fashion photographer, he rarely had call to wear such a sober outfit.

"The real luxury is to get something made for everyday life," he said.

So he got another suit made, only this time in burgundy-coloured corduroy: the coat was cut away at the bottom, giving a streamlined effect. "It was inspired by a picture of the Mallard steam train," Hills said with a grin. "I wanted it to be 'go-faster', but in a 1930s way."

It seemed all-too-obvious to point out that he seemed to like living in the past – but I pointed it out all the same.

He didn't disagree.

"I don't mind living in the past, relishing the heyday of men's clothing. Today, there are only two men's silhouettes – jeans and the suit. That's very boring. In the past, there were lots and lots of shapes." He flicked through a nearby book of suit designs through the ages, adding cheerfully: "My next suit is going to be a revival of the 1950s flare line."

To my surprise, he blames the boring state of most men's clothing on the regency dandy, Beau Brummell. "He was a real trendy," Hills agrees, "but he was responsible for making everyone wear black and white. He was responsible for the demise of colour, and fun, in men's clothes. And I would like to bring that back."

This is not about nostalgia, Hills said. "You don't want to look like a pastiche, or a fuddy duddy. My philosophy is ultra modern, it's about incorporating technology and so on. All my suits have a function. I wouldn't wear luminous plus fours if I wasn't cycling."

He didn't remember the exact price of his corduroy suit. But the cape, trousers and waistcoat he wore when I saw him at the school gates cost about £1,000 altogether. Plainly, Hills didn't mind spending a lot – in fact, he *preferred* to spend a lot.

"If you spend a lot of money, you look after things. If you buy something cheaply, you don't. People don't spend enough on clothes. I was talking to somebody recently, a taxi driver, who remembered that his father bought him a suit that cost two weeks' salary."

In a nutshell, he said, his philosophy is to have good things, and to wear them every day. It's a philosophy that I suggest fits well with being "green", and Hills agrees: "Prince Charles and Jonathan Porritt are two well-dressed beardy-weirdies."

Downstairs, in the basement, in a bedroom that hadn't been absolutely tidied up to the max, he showed me so many jackets and trousers and coats and shirts that I lost track. I hazily remember liking one that he called a scooter coat, with a vent at the back, based on coats worn by the Household Cavalry, with slots in the elbow for the insertion of what he called "elbow armour". And while Hills took calls about a forthcoming TV appearance, I played around with his sizeable collection of flat caps and a pair of reflective spats.

Then he took me upstairs, squeezing past bicycles and clothes racks, to show me roll after roll of his tweeds.

The idea to make his own tweeds occurred after he saw weaver Kirsty MacDougall's weaving show at the Royal College of Art. They talked, and Hills discovered that MacDougall couldn't afford to carry on after she graduated. So he persuaded his wife, a lawyer, to buy MacDougall a loom. Since then, she has sourced yarn and designed patterns to be woven in bulk in Scotland. In four years, they've produced about 800 metres. They made books of swatches, and Hills distributed these around Savile Row. He also got to know fashion students, who came up with slightly more bonkers ideas than the traditional tailors – including the cape and plus fours that can be let down into (fairly) ordinary looking trousers when Hills is not cycling.

These sell well in Japan, apparently, and in the US.

In the kitchen, Hills had shown me some hats he crocheted for his family. I wondered why he didn't make all his own suits too.

"I have always made things, and I love doing that. You've seen for yourself" – I'd told him about my home-made shirt – "that the pleasure of creating something is fantastic. But the more you do, the more you appreciate people doing things really well."

Before I left, I asked for a sample of "lumatwill" to show Harriet, and mentioned that she didn't always approve of me wearing certain items outside the house.

I suppose I shouldn't have been surprised to learn that his wife sometimes expressed similar objections his peculiar outfits – but I *was* surprised, because Hills dresses with such confidence.

"We are in this culture of the lowest common denominator," he said with some dismay. "And people do sometimes worry about looking smart. There is this idea that you have to dress for the group that you are joining.

"But there is a huge pleasure to be had in dressing up. My wife does sometimes say I can't go out dressed like that. But I do. I dress to please myself."

chapter 42

Harriet has her say

I am glad to report that something like this cheerfully self-confident attitude can pay dividends. I became aware of this after Harriet, who is also a writer, told me that she had been asked to write a magazine story about my shenanigans.

Here's what she wrote:

> In these difficult times, with the global economy in meltdown, you might think it would be a blessing to live with the master of thrift, the king of home-made, the god of mend and make do.
>
> But, boy, can my husband be annoying.
>
> I love luxury, and my antenna seem to be trained to seek out the most expensive things on offer. I shop at Liberty's, sneak off for tea at Claridge's, and like to loaf in fancy spas. So how did I find myself with someone who boils up mouldy vegetables to make stock, which he then ekes out over the rest of the week? Who raids skips for bits of wood he can turn into bookcases, takes our five year old daughter foraging for dandelion, nettle and lime leaves, and still keeps a pair of boxer shorts that are 20 years old.
>
> During the recent, bitterly cold snap, John-Paul nearly froze to death in his loft office at the top of our house, eschewing central heating in favour of a pair of fingerless mittens he'd made out of old socks. He wears two jumpers at once, not only to keep out the cold, but also because

this somewhat conceals the enormous holes, not perfectly overlapping, in the elbows. And he glues his knackered old trainers together to stop them from disintegrating. This week, I'm fighting a fierce battle to stop him appearing outside the house wearing a hat he knitted himself.

In every partnership, there is always one person who makes the decisions, if not about everything then at least in certain areas of life. We never discussed it in these terms, but it has always been my job to oversee our behaviour as consumers. Thus, I booked the holidays, chose the clothes (his as well as mine) and picked the restaurants. And for many years my husband was happy to go along with this.

For his own part, he has always been cheap to run. This has its blessings but, alas, it goes hand in hand with a lack of interest in making money. I should have seen it coming. We met at university in the late 80s just as Big Bang was promising to make millionaires of us all. While our contemporaries were dreaming of becoming bankers and corporate lawyers, he was going to be a poet.

It would be false to suggest that this irritated me. It may not have been very realistic but I found it endearing. After all, I studied English literature too. But his indifference to money and expense for their own sake is greater than mine, and we have waged a war over that disputed half-inch of territory ever since.

For instance, John-Paul has always had a tendency to get cheap and dodgy haircuts. Given half a chance, he would sneak off back to his childhood barber, who even now charges a fiver including tip – and if you had seen the results you'd not be surprised at the low price.

Before our daughter learned to speak, I announced that she would be having her haircut properly, at a salon of my choice. And soon afterwards I came home to find that John-Paul had inflicted his own inexpert scissor-work on her while I was at the office. I refused to talk to him for 24 hours.

This may seem like a small matter to you, but imagine what it's like to have a spouse – or a young child – whose appearance upsets you. Mercifully, when he agreed to be an usher at my sister's wedding, some years ago, I persuaded him to visit my own hairdresser, at John Frieda. It took months for him to stop muttering about the price, but he acknowledged the quality of the coffee.

I also gradually changed his taste in clothes. A decade ago, I persuaded him to buy a pair of hugely expensive Paper Denim & Cloth jeans. He admitted they were much more comfortable than his bargain-basement jeans, and infinitely cooler.

But it's all changed: he's no longer willing to go along with my expensive ways. He's gone back to cheap haircuts, and has just two pairs of jeans, one 'old' and one 'new' (even the new pair – almost five years old – is distressingly worn-out). He recently took apart the threadbare Paper Denim & Cloth jeans, already substantially patched, and bought a load of hemp denim with which to make a replica. He darns his socks while watching Newsnight, and saves the pips from every apple he eats (each pip, he tells me gleefully, is a possible tree).

As that last example hinted, John-Paul is not straightforwardly penny-pinching. In fact, he tends to be rather generous with tips, and drives me mad by failing to chase people who owe him money. No, his frugal attitude is largely down to his determination to 'step lightly' on the planet. But that doesn't make it any easier to live with. Under his influence, I have been stepping significantly more lightly myself, for some years now, but no matter how I may compare with others, I always feel like a lumbering flat-footed fool behind him. (He recently said, in response to somebody's complaints about carbon emissions from China, that I was a greater menace to the planet.)

Just when I've got my head around the fact that we need to conserve oil (not because it's expensive but because it's going to run out), John-Paul has moved on to the urgent need to conserve phosphorous, a mineral needed to grow food, which we flush thoughtlessly to sea. In fact, he's started to mutter about installing a composting loo, the ultimate thrift utility.

As I fill the fridge with delicious, ready-made puddings, he smiles the smile of the disappointed man. I know what he's thinking: that he'd rather I made them myself: he says he would love home-made pud, regardless of its flaws, just as he'd love it if I knitted him a jumper.

It's that sense of disappointment that gets me – the same disappointment I feel as he turns the lights off after me, or turns off the central heating while I sit by the roaring fire, or teaches me for the umpteenth time how to wash the dishes without keeping the hot tap running all the time.

A few years ago, he persuaded me we needed to buy an electric car – one of those tiny ones that so annoy Jeremy Clarkson. It has no suspension to speak of, and costs about 2p a day to run. I've grown to love it. But these days, I get that disappointed look every time I use it. Now, he says I should be riding a bike: a bike would be just as fast, he says, and I'd spend a lot less time working to pay the running costs.

This is one of his favourite speeches, and often leads to a peroration against the evil idea that 'time is money'. If I suggest that we should get somebody in to do something for us, he always says he could do whatever it is himself. If I say that he doesn't have the time, or could earn more doing something else, he points out that nobody is 'time rich', or 'time poor' because we've all got exactly 24 hours a day and we either choose to be busy or we don't.

He'd rather lead a life of variety, he says, and try his hand at unfamiliar tasks, than specialise for the sake of a marginally higher income.

This doesn't make it any easier when he offers to do whatever it is that needs doing himself. And he says that all the time.

I want new blinds for our conservatory. John-Paul says he can knock up just what we need using a few metres of fabric, possibly comprising old duvet covers, and six lengths of dowel from the hardware shop.

I want to get some pictures framed. Easy, he says, and pulls a saw and a mitre box from his little tool cupboard.

This week, I mentioned that I need a new pair of jeans: I'd found a lovely pair from J Brand, beloved of Kate Moss. Things being how they are, financially, I can hardly afford them – but I didn't expect him to say that he could make me those, too.

Ask him how he can justify this manic self-confidence, and he'll tell you about the time we were overrun by rats, two summers ago. To start with, we called Rentokil, as any sensible person would. But my husband got fed up waiting for them to turn up, and couldn't bring himself to pay the admittedly rather large fees, so he decided to tackle the pests himself.

He bought a kind of elasticated miners' lamp to wear on his head, and some thick gloves, and crawled below the floorboards to do battle with our own little Rolands. He was very successful, and so far hasn't succumbed to Weil's Disease.

It was the same story with the fitted book-shelves. We got some carpenters in to give us a quote – and believe me, even getting him to agree to that was hard enough – but they didn't come back to us for weeks, so he found some wood in a skip and put up a bookcase himself. As with our daughter's haircut, he did this while I was at work, so that I only found out once the job was done, and couldn't prevent it.

The annoying thing is that he is actually rather skilled – except at children's haircuts – and sickeningly inspiring. When he puts his mind to it, he really does prove that it is possible for a novice to turn out a decent picture frame, run a successful allotment and fashion a chair out of an old crate. And when it comes down to it, isn't that a bit more attractive than a man who calls in the electrician to change a plug?

It seemed bonkers a decade ago, and deeply frustrating. Even last year, his outlook would by most people have been deemed quirky. But with the economy, and the climate, in meltdown, it seems – and I'm grinding my jaws as I type this – that his time has come.

chapter 43

Should a man crochet in public?

In her book *Knitting for Good*, the American writer Betsy Greer describes how knitting gradually became more than just a way to pass the time, or create her own garments. "It calmed me, it connected me, it inspired me, it soothed me with the repetitive movements that also symbolised the growth of a garment or an accessory, each stitch simultaneously a push forward and a mark of time."

I've come to feel the same way, and seen for myself just how soothing this kind of work can be – a pleasure in its own right.

Eventually Greer sought out knitting groups and took to knitting in public. Indeed, her first experience of doing that was in London, where she was living in 2003, with Rachel Matthews and her Cast Off Knitting Club.

Be the change you want to see in the world, Gandhi said, and he demonstrated what he had in mind by spinning at political meetings. Greer had a similar idea in mind when she coined the term "craftivism". The word spells out what should be obvious but is often overlooked: that each time you participate in crafting you are making a difference. "Craft is a way of rejoicing, passing time, meditating, harnessing power, sharing and keeping creative forces in motion," as she puts it. "Because it is possible to go beyond banners, email petitions and chants as ways of fighting for a cause you believe in."

So if I was really going to Be The Change perhaps I too needed to get out there and knit or crochet in public.

But something held me back.

There's a big difference between me and Greer, or indeed Matthews, as Greer's book makes only too clear, in passages about how feminists today are embracing what earlier feminists shunned: a women's tradition. At a time when women are expected to shoot through the glass ceiling at work, and no area of work is out of bounds, clothes-making remains unaccountably inaccessible to men (except at the very highest levels, e.g., on the catwalks). As I've found in books and in shops, people just don't expect it to interest us.

Sure, I can claim to be descended from a lot of women, and I have only one child – a daughter – which might make it easier to do crochet than if I had (say) five sons. But should I really go on the tube to crochet? Should I go somewhere else? Would I be wise to knit only "manly" yarns and patterns? If so, what might they be?

I contacted Greer, in search of some answers. After thinking about it for several weeks, she sent a long and thoughtful reply.

"I'm sorry to say that the whole dude thing and knitting must, honestly, kind of suck," she wrote with evident sympathy.

More generally though, she wondered what exactly I wanted to achieve. "What 'change' are you specifically trying to be? The change behind making your own clothes? Starting dialogue? Encouraging public creativity? Because in my opinion, if you're looking to start a conversation regarding the clothing industry, you might want to consider knitting somewhere like Carnaby Street." (Greer used to live in London.)

"Taking your knitting to a place like this, where it's not the East End and trendy, where people will come up to you and ask you what the crap you're doing because they haven't seen anyone knitting since the 60s, will strike up a discussion around what we wear and how it came to be.

"Knitting on the Tube is awesome, and def recommended as it's fun, but given the fact it's transportation and getting people from point A to point B, it might be harder to engage in an actual discussion. I might be tempted to print out some sort of brochure related to the history of men knitting to hand out to naysayers."

In conclusion, Greer could hardly have been more encouraging: "I think it's great what you're doing! But with a field so rich and interdisciplinary and historic it's freakin' hard to pinpoint the heart of the matter sometimes... Craft's beauty and utility can bring out the beast in the form of a million questions – that lead to a million more."

chapter 44

Ancient woollen underpants

A possible answer to (some of) those questions came up after a morning reading Rachel Matthews amusing Prick Your Finger blog. After reading quirky stories about, among other things, a boggy region in France where shepherds used to sit on a tripod of stilts to keep their feet dry and knit till it was home-time, I came across some very useful web links.

One of these directed me to a set of instructions on how to unravel old woollen items and reuse the yarn. You might not think there's a lot to it, but believe me, it's a complicated business, and the instructions have won plaudits from net-savvy knitters worldwide.

The writer turned out to be an American mother of five children, living in Colorado. She has a virtual shop on Etsy, the online craft site, called The Twice Sheared Sheep. I checked it out, and got in touch. I congratulated her on what she's doing, and put in a request for certain balls of forest-green wool, with which I hoped to make, I dunno, a sleeveless sweater. But I was worried that buying it from somebody so far away went against the recycling ethos.

A few hours later, she replied: "I am so glad that you like my yarn. I don't think that shipping all over the world is contrary to the whole recycling thing. It allows more people to experience the joy :) I'm afraid that the green bulky wool is not going to be enough for a tank top or vest. I have a gigantic sweater stash at the moment, though, and would be happy to rifle through it and see if I have what you are looking for. Looking at various free online patterns, I think you will probably need about 1000 yards of worsted weight yarn. Is this a vest to wear over another shirt, or a tank top to wear alone? Do you knit or crochet? What colours were you looking for?"

I was daunted by the questions, because I didn't know the answers. In the end, I said I might try to crochet the thing, because then I could do it simply in one piece, rather than do separate front and back that might not fit together when it came to making it up.

She replied again: "Your plan on how to construct a crochet vest sounds right on. Crochet can be more flexible about things like that than knitting. Crochet also sucks up a lot more yarn than knitting, though, and produces a thicker, warmer fabric... I have another sweater that is almost exactly the same as this one, just a touch lighter green. It should produce enough yarn for the project you have in mind if you would like me to bump that to the top of the list."

I asked her to go ahead, and thought for a while about how I might feel crocheting a manly sweater on London Underground.

Another link from Rachel Matthews' blog led me to an amazing woman in Norway – a weaving teacher, Annemor Sundbø, who set out to investigate the rich history of handmade garments in the stockpile of a recycled wool factory and ended up taking over the business.

Since then, she's published several books about what she had found, and it seemed that everybody in the online knitting universe who has heard of Sundbø just loves those books.

I sent off for my own copies, and when they arrived I was gripped by her stories of finding treasure in the ragpile.

"I found a striking example of a ladies' long johns," she writes near the beginning of her first book, *Everyday Knitting*. "The contrast to the modern g-string was indescribable."

She could say that again. To judge by the photographs, the long-johns were made out of an old sweater that had been cut up and resewn, and patched all over many times.

"They were originally knitted as a fisherman's gansey, with cable-pattern using homespun yarn. The wool might have come from one of the owner's own sheep. Carding and spinning probably took about one week, and the yarn was dyed with fermented urine and indigo.

"The pattern is complicated and time consuming, maybe made as an engagement present, which the owner proudly wore for many years. But after years of use and careful mending, one day enough was enough. The gansey was turned upside down and made into warm underwear for a cold day during the Second World War."

Old fashioned long underwear of this kind is virtually forgotten, Sundbø writes.

"Most of what we know about underwear fashions of the past is from old-fashioned magazines and catalogues, but the everyday underwear of the countryside is not mentioned. It is difficult to find information about underwear in literary sources and folklore traditions. There are only a few undergarments in museum collections, probably because people didn't usually dig out their old underwear to give to museums."

It's important to note that these unmentionables (as Sundbø terms them) were not exactly worn with pride, even at the time. She mentions a traveller writing in the 1800s who was shocked by women dancing at a wedding.

"He described their skirts as looking like loose sails in a storm He was also shocked to discover that they wore nothing under their skirts. When asked to dance by one of the women, he declined. When she persisted, he replied that he was embarrassed by the fact that these immodest women didn't cover their bodies properly.

"The woman laughed, and said she wouldn't have dared to turn up at a dance wearing her self-made and repaired underwear, and forever after be teased by the boys. It was better to show off what God had created.

"I found solid evidence in the ragpile that the girls were using underwear of a most substantial nature, and I quite understand that sometimes it might have been easier to bear the shame of doing without!"

chapter 45

The kingdom of heaven is within you

If you are concerned about protecting the environment, and moving towards a life that is sustainable, you soon find yourself accused of wishing to turn the clock back – trying to "return to the Stone Age" or, slightly less drastic, the Middle Ages.

In case there is any doubt, it should be stressed that the people who make these accusations do not regard a return to the Middle Ages as a good idea. Some of them regard life before the so-called Enlightenment as almost a different order of existence altogether, and certainly an inferior one.

Typically, they point to the harsher elements of medieval life – plague, poverty, serfdom, and war, forgetting that those dreadful ills still exist today.

Plague: more died of flu, in 1918, than were wiped out by the First World War. There's still no cure for Aids, and the menace of avian flu spreading death around the world hangs over us all.

Poverty: the gap between rich and poor in the UK has got bigger and bigger. Poverty can never be eliminated, because rich and poor are relative terms, like north and south: you can't have one without the other. To put that another way: your money would be worthless if your neighbour had no lack of it.

Serfdom: most serfs live overseas, these days, working out of sight and out of mind in the sweatshops that produce our cheap goods. But some live in the UK, where they are exploited in the sex trade.

War: we still have war, and we have made it worse than ever. In the past, only 10 per cent of the victims were civilians and 90 per cent were soldiers – now, it's the other way round.

Additionally, sceptics present crude parodies of medieval belief systems for ridicule.

This deserves some consideration. It's my belief that unfamiliar modes of thought can be more subtle than our own, or considerably more vivid, while essentially conveying much the same thing.

Take allegory, in which abstract nouns are embodied as living beings. Rarely used today, allegory was used extensively in the Middle Ages to get across complex ideas.

For instance: things that seem harmless in themselves can, at a certain remove or huge scale, become terrifyingly harmful. The American novelist John Steinbeck, in *The Grapes of Wrath*, made clear that the banks that foreclosed loans and caused such suffering during the Great Depression were staffed with people who, almost without exception, hated what the bank was doing. But they did it anyway, because the "emergent properties" of the banking system called on them to do so. The ecologist Alastair McIntosh, in his book *Soil and Soul*, takes Steinbeck's point further by suggesting that these emergent properties are fundamentally unavoidable in any human system, and might possibly be what previous generations had in mind when they talked of "the devil' – an anthropomorphic embodiment of what today we choose to conceal behind rather less vivid abstract nouns.

Now, I find it as hard as the next person to take seriously the medieval idea of the devil, but it seems only fair to our predecessors to point out that we, too, cling to ideas that may come to be seen as laughable by our descendents.

One of the most toxic specimens of contemporary received wisdom is the idea of "progress" itself, embraced vigorously since the early 19th century by capitalists and Marxists alike. Still today, most people would regard you as mad if you suggested that the drive for progress should be halted. But some free-thinking individuals have started to put the idea under scrutiny, shedding light on what has been called the "progress trap' – a condition societies experience when, in pursuing progress, human ingenuity inadvertently introduces problems that the society does not have the resources to solve.

Thus in the early Stone Age, improved hunting techniques caused the extinction of many prey species. The alternative, agriculture, in time proved even more trap-prone. Almost any sphere of technology can prove a progress trap, even medicine: for example, eliminating natural selection is causing an increase in genetic risks.

In worst cases, the progress trap leads to the collapse of entire civilisations: the classic case would be Easter Island, where all trees were cut down for transporting stone monuments. Today, unabated oil consumption in the face of climate change seems chillingly similar.

The people who revile the Middle Ages tend to overlook many great pleasures that were available in the past, even more readily than they are today. Not least among these were the opportunity to engage with unspoiled nature, to grow your own food, and to make your own clothes, rather than meekly absorb somebody else's efforts.

I don't doubt that for people accustomed to the luxuries of the 21st century, a return to medieval conditions would be shockingly uncomfortable, but it seems pretty clear to me, having studied key texts from the new Positive Psychology, and also the ancient teachings of the Buddha, that people in the Middle Ages had just as much scope for happiness as we do today – and also for unhappiness.

Thich Nhat Hanh put the point clearly in a recent book. After visiting the west in 1966 to call for an end to the war in Vietnam, he was refused the right to return. He was cut off from all his friends and students, and almost every night he dreamed of going home.

"During that time I practiced mindfulness diligently. I practiced to be in touch with children and adults in Europe and America. I learned to contemplate the trees and the singing of the birds. Everything seemed different from what we knew in Vietnam. And yet the wonders of life were available to me in these new lands, too. I came to the realisation that, with the practice of mindfulness, my true home can be found everywhere on this planet.

"I became aware that the Kingdom of God, the Pure Land of the Buddha, the place of true peace depends on our own capacity to wake up to all the wonders of life that surround us right in this moment, in this place. It is possible for us to touch the Kingdom of God every day. It is possible, and it is up to us to do it. I often tell my students, come back and claim your true inheritance. Return to your true home, in the here and now. With just one mindful step, with just one mindful breath, we can find ourselves in our paradise."

So by making clothes you can experience the Kingdom of Heaven right now.

This, certainly, was the lesson I took from yet another inspiring American, the Rev Callie Janoff. As a child, Janoff learned to meditate but was otherwise not much interested in the spiritual life until one day, in conversation with friends she was confronted with the questions: "What in your life is spiritual?" and "If I'm a spiritual person how does that express itself in my life?"

They all came to the same answer: making things. "When we make things we are connecting to the part of ourselves that we imagine is the spiritual part, the part most resembling divinity."

With one particular friend, she decided to set up a whole new religion. "We dreamed of a church that really could embrace a diversity of outlooks on spirituality, even atheism. We decided to call it The Church of Craft."

Meetings started out playfully, with talk about specific projects, then led to deeper discussion. "Our making was becoming more important than the products of our craft. Artists who created for a living would come and just play, without worrying about whether what they made would sell. People who didn't think of themselves as artists could give themselves permission to try something that intimidated them, because it didn't matter if what they made turned out as planned."

Soon people were contacting Janoff from all over the US and around the world, asking for permission to set up their own chapters – permission she readily granted.

Janoff has learned a lot from the Church of Craft. "I've learned that in our capitalist society bigger isn't always better: a meeting is still great and serves its purpose if only one or two people show up. Growth and progress are also mirages of accomplishment; being present here and now are the things we really need to worry about. Consumption eats self-esteem; creation makes it grow. I've written and said this so many times, but I believe it strongly: making things makes us happier, more whole people."

Does it also help to resolve wider problems? I think it does.

I recently went to a dinner party in a part of London where it seems that everybody drives a 4×4. I sat next to a woman who listened politely as I described some of the things I have been up to, to minimise climate change and prepare for peak oil.

I thought I might get a sympathetic hearing, because this was a woman who works for a liberal newspaper, more lefty and earnestly well-meaning than mine – or so most people probably believe.

But she took me aback by announcing that there was "no point" doing what I was doing. I would be better off lobbying the UN, she said, or the government. Then she changed tack, admitting that climate change and energy issues leave her feeling hopeless. "Just look at India and China," she said, meaning presumably that they are becoming bigger users of energy all the time, and that making your own shirt in London is neither here nor there.

This was demoralising, but her point was easy enough to refute. If we do nothing we are really in trouble, whereas we might just make a difference by taking action. If your car is heading for a cliff and the prospect of falling alarms you, you don't for that reason say there's no point applying the brake – far less lobby the government to tell you to apply it.

Like many people, this woman was paralysed by the scale of the problems facing us, combined with the urgency. She should relax: we can't do everything at once. We can make a great deal of change incrementally. And there's nothing we can do *except* as individuals.

So, my project to make an entire outfit myself is good for me, and it's good for the world. It's good for *you*.

And as the final part of that project I have decided to make my own underpants.

After all, this journey started with me wearing nothing but pants, back inside that felt-lined laser-chamber at Brooks Brothers. And I only finally recognised how quality is systematically impaired by the global clothing industry when Jeremy Paxman complained about his shoddy M&S briefs. And what better way to address the idea that clothes making is "women's work" than by making a pair of Y-fronts?

But how to do it?

As a first step, I cut up an old woollen sweater and turned it into a pair of pants like the ones worn till recently in Norway (and perhaps more widely). It was not too difficult to work out the pattern, based on the pants that Asha had bought for me.

The result was quite good, but incredibly itchy. Perhaps this was a good thing: wearing the pants could be a kind of penance for thinking it was funny to ask Asha to buy my pants back when I was outsourcing my life.

But I wasn't quite happy yet. I felt that John Ruskin would have liked my pants even more if I'd really customised them, in tribute to his beloved Gothic stonemasons. How to do that? I set to work with my fabric pen. On one side of the Y, I drew Jeremy Clarkson, and on the other a figure representing Rebecca Lush. Flying across the middle I drew a custard pie. This represented the Buddhist concept of the interconnectedness of all things: for as long as those pants endure, Clarkson and Lush will be together.

But still I wasn't entirely satisfied. These pants were to be the crowning glory in my outfit – invisible to other people, but no less important to me for all that.

What I had made was fine, but what if I made Y-fronts from scratch? I looked in my by now sizeable "stash" of yarn for a ball of undyed nettle and started to crochet, using a relatively small hook because otherwise my pants would be full of holes and basically see-through in a way that many people, me included, might regard as *not good*.

To begin, I crocheted only into the back of each stitch to get a ribbed, naturally elasticated effect: this would keep the pants from falling down, I hoped. Alas, it was a bit lacy, which meant I must either use a smaller needle, which could double the time required to make the pants, or use thicker yarn, which would be faster but would result in very warm, not to say hot, pants.

I opted for thicker yarn: glossy wool from a breed of sheep called blue-faced Leicester.

Working only into the front of each stitch again, I made the band around the bottom of each leg, then very slowly worked to join the bits together to the body of the pants. As I did the work, I thought of all the people who had inspired me to make this journey, too many to mention by name. I went over them all by category, as I'd learned to do from the Anglican prayer site: close friends and relations, teachers, people with power, the powerless and the poor, and finally myself.

When that got boring I did it again using a Buddhist technique for projecting loving-kindness by turns towards oneself, a loved one, somebody we feel basically indifferent towards, and finally anyone who annoys the hell out of us.

I also thought every so often of something written by that same Joanna Macy whose quote I'd seen on the back of Thich Nhat Hahn's book. This addressed my long-standing concern that enjoying the moment was, in practice, an irresponsible distraction from trying to resolve all the big problems facing us. Macy put it the other way round: "When we stop distracting ourselves by trying to figure the chances of success or failure, our minds and heart are liberated into the present moment. This moment then becomes alive, charged with possibilities, as we realise how lucky we are to be alive now, to take part in this planetary adventure." And, specifically, to crochet our own undergarments.

The crochet took several evenings, and was carried out in front of Harriet but without her being absolutely aware of what I was up to.

Then one day, when Harriet had gone to work, I finished the crocheted pants and put them on.

They were still, I confess, a bit see-through, and barely less itchy than the woollen pants made from my old felted jumper. But nobody needed to know that – so long as I didn't get involved in a traffic accident and rushed to hospital.

Feeling tremendously pleased with myself, I put on my home-made shirt and home-made jeans, then a hat I had crocheted using old carrier bags, which had been photographed to illustrate Harriet's magazine story about me.

No: this was wrong. I took off the hat, and also the jeans. Even the Savile Row trousers wouldn't do. I had made the pants, and that was enough. The rest of my outfit would be stylish, and didn't need to be home-made. Wearing nothing but hand-made pants, I dashed upstairs to the cupboard in my office and pulled out what had still never yet been seen outside the house: one of my Brooks Brothers suits.

I pulled on the trousers, buttoned the jacket, and slipped on a pair of shoes I'd repaired previously with glue.

And then I stepped outside into the sunshine, the kingdom of heaven bursting out all over.

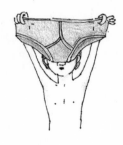

ACKNOWLEDGEMENTS

I couldn't have written this book without many, many people giving me their time – a good number of them mentioned in this book, and others whose books gave me ideas (see Further Reading).

Then there are the many editors who commissioned me (and in one case, Harriet) to write about some of the subjects in this book, and the other editors and photographers and illustrators and designers and publicists who helped to present my (and her) words to good effect. I'm truly, deeply grateful to them all, but owe a particular debt to Anna Guyer and Joe McAllister for quite extraordinarily generous help.

My family and friends have been utterly supportive too, but most especially Nancy and Harriet.

Thank you everybody.

FURTHER READING

This is a list of some of the books I read while writing this one. Do please try them.

Batmanghelidjh, Camila, *Shattered Lives*, Jessica Kingsley Publishers. Founder of Kids Company on some of the children whose lives she has helped to rebuild.

Bell, Graham, *The Permaculture Garden*, Permanent Publications. Unbeatable and inspiring guide to using permaculture at home. Great bibliography too.

Berry, Wendell, *The Art Of The Commonplace*, Counterpoint. Brilliant "agrarian essays" that stress the value of a relationship to the soil, wherever you find yourself.

Burnett, Graham, *Earth Writings*, Spiralseed. Charming and inspiring book, illustrated and published by Burnett himself.

Canfor-Dumas, Edward, *The Buddha, Geoff And Me*, Random House. Canfor-Dumas somehow manages to make a gripping novel about one ordinary Londoner's discovery of Buddhism.

Childish, Billy, *Paintings Of A Backwater Visionary*, The Aquarium; *The Man With The Gallows Eyes: Selected poetry 1980-2005*, Aquarium. Full of vim, or absolutely unlimited pffft!, as the painter-poet says himself.

Cormack, Trenna, *Be The Change*, Love Books. Interviews with several brilliant individuals trying to make a big difference.

Cutler, Ivor, *Befriend A Bacterium*, Pickpockets; *Life In A Scotch Sitting Room*, Methuen. Almost impossible to describe Cutler's take on the world – often funny, sweet, quirky and touching, if not all at once.

Fern, Ken, *Plants For A Future*, Permanent Publications. Former London bus driver went to Cornwall to grow hundreds, probably thousands of overlooked plants that can often be eaten and have other valuable uses too.

Ferriss, Timothy, *The 4-Hour Work Week*, Vermillion. Among other tips, author recommends that you log onto email only once or twice a week, and rarely turn on phone, so that people stop bothering you unnecessarily.

Fischer, Louis, *The Life of Mahatma Gandhi*, Harper Collins. Lively and readable account of the Mahatma by American journalist who knew him pretty well. Not overwhelmingly detailed on spinning and weaving, but Richard Attenborough says reading it changed his life.

Fukuoka, Masanobu, *The One-Straw Revolution*, Other India Press. Fukuoka, a former plant scientist, concluded with good evidence that there was little point interfering in natural processes, in almost any way at all, and achieved high yields without even digging. Quiet, modest, and utterly revolutionary.

Greer, Betsy, *Knitting For Good!*, Trumpeter. The original craftivist, Greer recognised that protesting with a beautifully knitted banner is better than using ugly, ill-made signs.

Hatton, Jean, *Betsy: The dramatic biography of prison reformer Elizabeth Fry*. Shows that even Fry didn't find it easy.

Hodgkinson, Tom, *How To Be Free*, Penguin. Manifesto urging us to throw off the shackles of modern life and enjoy ourselves.

Hollins, Arthur, *The Farmer, The Plough And The Devil*, Ellingham Press. In a lifelong experiment, Hollins learned to stop ploughing his land and let the soil improve itself – to the amazement of his neighbours.

Hopkins, Rob, *The Transition Handbook*, Green Books. Bible of the Transition Town movement, examining evidence of climate change and peak oil and prescribing variety of upbeat, locally-based solutions.

Huxley, Aldous (introduction), *Bhagavad-Gita: The song of God*, Signet Classics. Beautiful translation by Swami Prabhavandanda and Christopher Isherwood.

Ingram, Catherine, *In The Footsteps Of Gandhi*, Parallax Press. Joanna Macey, Thich Nhat Hanh and others on how they have been inspired by the Mahatma.

Jacobs, AJ, *The Year Of Living Biblically*, Arrow Books. Jacobs lives by the Bible for 12 months with results that are funny but also genuinely thought-provoking.

Knight, India, *The Thrift Book: Live well, spend less*, Fig Tree. Brilliantly and cheerfully captures the resourceful spirit of our times, and promises that thrifty measures can be their own reward.

Kornfield, Jack (editor), *Teachings Of The Buddha*, Shambhala. Translations of various Buddhist sources, not all of them immediately accessible to beginners.

Lane, John, *Timeless Simplicity*, Green Books. History and philosophy of the simple life. Impossible not to feel inspired towards owning less, after reading this, and relying more on your own resources. Beautifully illustrated too.

Layard, Richard, *Happiness*, Penguin. Professor at the London School of Economics points out that happiness doesn't come from accumulation of possessions and hints at where it may be found.

Levine, Faythe and Heimerl, Cortney, *Handmade Nation*, Princeton Architectural Press. Beautifully illustrated account of various crafty people across the US, with essays and manifestos from some of the foremost of them.

Lewis, Martin (editor), *Thrifty Ways For Modern Days*, Vermillion. Not exactly inspiring but contains substantial number of unglamorous money-saving tips.

Maathai, Wangari, *Unbowed: One Woman's Story*, William Heinemann. Startling insights into the ongoing effects of colonialism in Kenya, from former Nobel Peace prize winner.

Mabey, Richard, *Food For Free*, Collins Gem. Since reading this have been unable to step outside house without eating something growing wild.

Matthews, Rachael, *Hookorama: 25 fabulous things to crochet*, MQ Publications. I've not actually used many of the ideas in here but been inspired by them to try all kinds of things of my own, including a family of crocheted bears, and innumerable flowers.

McDonough, William and Braungart, Michael, *Cradle To Cradle*, North Point Press. Call to arms to designers and manufacturers to make reuse and recycling routine.

McIntosh, Alastair, *Hell and High Water: Climate change, hope and the human condition*, Birlinn; *Soil and Soul: People versus corporate power*, Aurum. McIntosh tells wonderful stories, and draws insights from huge range of sources. Most valuable, and unfashionable, is his take on biblical prophets: makes them seem like so many George Monbiots.

Moss, Stephen, *The Bumper Book Of Nature*, Square Peg. Author was planning a book about various things going wrong with nature, but decided instead to do one about what's right about it. And what a book!

Murphy, Bernardette, *Zen and the Art of Knitting*, Adams Media. One woman's account of learning to knit, and the therapeutic effect it had. This book provided pattern for the two-legged elephant I knitted for Nancy.

Nhat Hanh, Thich, *The Miracle of Mindfulness*, Rider; *Peace Is Every Step*, Rider; *The Heart Of The Buddha's Teaching*, Rider. You don't have to be a Buddhist to find useful lessons and encouragement in these books. Absolutely and utterly recommended, though beginners may not want to bother with *The Heart Of The Buddha's Teaching*.

Norberg-Hodge, Helena, *Ancient Futures*, Random House. Norberg-Hodge has spent decades in Ladakh watching the sustainable, traditional way of life being eroded by outside influence. Frankly and refreshingly argues for a return to (much of) the past.

Norman, Jill, *Make Do And Mend*, Michael O'Mara. Official Second World War leaflets ("for housewives") on how to darn and patch threadbare clothes, among other things.

Price, Dan, *Radical Simplicity*, Running Press. Price, a latter-day Thoreau, on living in variety of self-made shelters.

Quaker Faith And Practice, Religious Society of Friends. Contains the useful "Advices and Queries" - as close to a credo as anything the Quakers have. ("Take heed, dear friends, to the promptings of love and truth in your heart…") Also variously consoling and inspiring insights from Quakers alive and dead, in UK and around the world.

Readers Digest Complete DIY Manual, Readers Digest. It's all there: plumbing, carpentry, you name it.

Reynolds, Richard, *On Guerrilla Gardening*, Bloomsbury. Reynolds has done more to inspire planting in public spaces than anybody since the 16th century Diggers.

Rosen, Nick, *How to Live Off-Grid*, Bantam Books. Author meets people who, like him, are trying to detach themselves from the electrical grid, and indeed any other grid you care to name.

Rowden, Sarah and Vestey, Joanna, *Custard And Crayons With Polly And Jago*, Wigwam Press. Sweet, beautifully illustrated book full of artsy-crafty things to do with young people (or, if you prefer, without).

Ruskin, John, *Unto This Last And Other Writings*, Penguin. The essay that changed Gandhi's life.

Schumacher, EF, *Small Is Beautiful: A study of economics as if people mattered*, Abacus. Challenges doctrine of specialisation and proposes smaller working units, communal ownership and regional workplaces using local labour and resources.

Scott Cato, Molly, *Green Economics*, Earthscan. Well argued and provocative account of sustainable economics includes investigation into the value of a locally made hat.

Seymour, John, *Self-Sufficiency*, Dorling Kindersley. There's not much left out of this practical guide to making do on your own.

Sims, Andrew and Smith, Joe (editors), *Do Good Lives Have To Cost The Earth*, Constable. Essays by, among others, Phillip Pullman, Colin Tudge, and Anne Pettifor.

Smith, Adam, *The Wealth of Nations*, OUP. Look out for the author's acknowledgement that division of labour brutalises the workers.

Sundbo, Annemor, *Everyday Knitting: Treasures from a ragpile*, Torridal Tweed; *Invisible Threads in Knitting*, Torridal Tweed. Extraordinary insights into how people used to make own clothes – including pants fashioned from old pullovers.

The Bible (King James Version), OUP. You've heard of this one already.

Tolstoy, Leo, *The Kingdom Of God and Peace Essays*, OUP. Forceful and heartfelt essays urging people to adopt Christ's teachings whether or not they belong to churches – in fact, better not.

Wallace, Danny, *Join Me*, Ebury; *Random Acts of Kindness: 365 ways to make the world a nicer place*, Ebury. Man who started cult by accident, and some of the lovely things his followers have done.

Warren, Piers, *101 Uses For Stinging Nettles*, Wildeye; *British Native Trees: Their past and present uses*, Wildeye. Titles tell you all you need to know.

Whitefield, Patrick, *Permaculture In a Nutshell*, Permanent Publications; *The Earth Care Manual*, Permanent Publications. Take your pick: the short version or the stunningly comprehensive overview. Every library should have a copy of each.

Wiseman, Ann Sayre, *The Best Of Making Things*, Hand Print Press. The best possible guide to widest possible range of crafting projects, with easy-to-follow instructions and charming line drawings.

Wright, Ronald, *An Illustrated Short History of Progress*, Anansi. Elegant and learned discussion showing how several past civilisations rendered their own way of life obsolete and destroyed themselves.

Inspiration for Self Reliance

books that make a difference from Permanent Publications

Plants For A Future, Ken Fern

Like Richard Mabey's Food for Free, this book has the potential absolutely to revolutionise our approach to eating. Contains charming anecdotes and useful facts on trees, woodland plants, edible flowers, pond and bog gardening, edible lawns and growing on walls and fences.
£16.95. 344pp. Over 60 photos & 2 illustrations

Permaculture In A Nutshell, Patrick Whitefield

The best possible introduction to the ideas behind permaculture, which applies to so much more than just food growing. Whitefield, one of the best known practitioners and teachers, briskly outlines the principles, and how to apply them in practice - in the city, the garden, on the farm and in the community.
£5.95. 96pp. 14 line drawings

The Permaculture Garden, Graham Bell

Even the smallest back yard can be transformed into a beautiful and highly productive garden, as this much loved guide demonstrates. It shows how to plan for maximum yields with minimal labour, to save money and resources.
£14.95. 170pp. 250 photos & 65 line drawings & tables

The Woodland House (Second Edition), Ben Law

The story of how Ben designed and built his iconic woodland house. Voted the greatest ever Grand Design (by Channel 4 viewers) this proves it's possible to design and construct a truly environmental friendly home. With seven year update.
£14.95. 104pp. Over 100 photos & many drawings/plans

The Earth Care Manual, Patrick Whitefield

Truly awesome bible of permaculture as suited to Britain and other places with temperate climates. Contains in-depth analysis and detailed advice relating to soil, climate, water, energy, buildings, gardens, farming, woodland and the design process.
£39.95. 480pp. 250 photos & many diagrams/illustrations

available from all good bookshops

www.permaculture.co.uk

If You Enjoyed This Book
You Won't Want to Miss
This Magazine!

Permaculture Magazine helps you live a more natural, healthy and environmentally friendly life.

Permaculture Magazine offers tried and tested ways of creating flexible, low cost approaches to sustainable living. It can help you to:

- Make informed ethical choices
- Grow and source organic food
- Help you resource ethical clothing
- Put more into your local community
- Build energy efficiency into your home
- Find courses, contacts and opportunities
- Live in harmony with people and the planet

Permaculture Magazine is published quarterly for enquiring minds and original thinkers everywhere. Each issue gives you practical, thought provoking articles written by leading experts as well as fantastic eco-friendly tips from readers!

**permaculture, ecovillages, organic gardening, sustainable agriculture, agroforestry, appropriate technology, eco-building, downshifting, community development, human-scale economy...
and much more!**

Permaculture Magazine gives you access to a unique network of people and introduces you to pioneering projects in Britain and around the world. Subscribe today and start enriching your life without overburdening the planet!

Every issue of *Permaculture Magazine* brings you the best ideas, advice and inspiration from people who are working towards a more sustainable world.

Permanent Publications
The Sustainability Centre, East Meon, Hampshire GU32 1HR, UK
Tel: 0845 458 4150 or 01730 823 311 Fax: +44 (0)1730 823 322
Email: orders@permaculture.co.uk Web: www.permaculture.co.uk